THE SEVEN GREAT UNTENABLES

THE SEVEN GREAT
UNTENABLES

(*Sapta-vidhā Anupapatti*)

JOHN GRIMES

MOTILAL BANARSIDASS PUBLISHERS
PRIVATE LIMITED • DELHI

First Edition: Delhi, 1990

ISBN: 81–208–0682–4

Also available at:
MOTILAL BANARSIDASS
41 U.A., Bungalow Road, Jawahar Nagar, Delhi 110 007
120 Royapettah High Road, Mylapore, Madras 600 004
24 Race Course Road, Bangalore 560 001
Ashok Rajpath, Patna 800 004
Chowk, Varanasi 221 001

PRINTED IN INDIA
BY JAINENDRA PRAKASH JAIN AT SHRI JAINENDRA PRESS, A-45 NARAINA INDUSTRIAL AREA, PHASE I, NEW DELHI 110 028 AND PUBLISHED BY NARENDRA PRAKASH JAIN FOR MOTILAL BANARSIDASS PUBLISHERS PVT. LTD., BUNGALOW ROAD, JAWAHAR NAGAR, DELHI 110 007

To my teacher

Professor R. Balasubramanian

in appreciation of his guidance and

my association with

Radhakrishnan Institute of

Advanced Study in Philosophy

FOREWORD

Ramanuja raised seven major objections against the Advaita conception of *avidyā*. He brings in, under each one of these objections, further objections which, if valid, will prove the Advaita conception of *avidyā* untenable. As well, post-Ramanuja scholars took up the sword and attempted to finish the dialectics. This book is an analysis of these objections and rejoinders to them from an Advaitic perspective.

The work consists of seven chapters with notes and select bibliography and falls into identifiable parts. Grimes covers a wide range of ideas connected with basic Vedantic positions vis-a-vis Advaita and Visistadvaita. This itself is creditable.

The work is clearly written and organized. Each argument is clearly presented and responded to. As well, there is a good summary of key Vedantic ideas and arguments concerning the concept of *avidyā*. As a handbook regarding the debate over the status of *avidyā*, it will be found useful.

Though the polemics between Advaitins and Visistadvaitins is unending, the conflicts which exist between the two systems does not seem to affect their value as particular approaches to Brahman. One may even go so far as to say that the two systems enrich and inspire each other with a mutual fecundity.

P.K. SUNDARAM

SCHEME OF TRANSLITERATION

अ	a	आ	ā	इ	i	ई	ī		
उ	u	ऊ	ū	ऋ	ṛ	ॠ	ṝ		
लृ	ḷ	ए	e	ऐ	ai	ओ	o		
औ	au	अं	aṁ	अः	aḥ				
क्	k	ख्	kh	ग्	g	घ्	gh	ङ्	ṅ
च्	c	छ्	ch	ज्	j	झ्	jh	ञ्	ñ
ट्	ṭ	ठ्	ṭh	ड्	ḍ	ढ्	ḍh	ण्	ṇ
त्	t	थ्	th	द्	d	ध्	dh	न्	n
प्	p	फ्	ph	ब्	b	भ्	bh	म्	m
य्	y	र्	r	ल्	l	व्	v		
श्	ś	ष्	ṣ	स्	s	ह्	h		
ळ्	ḷ	क्ष्	kṣ	त्र्	tr	ज्ञ्	jñ		

CONTENTS

Pages

Foreword vii
Scheme of Transliteration viii
Preface xiii

Chapter One—INTRODUCTION

1. Introduction to the Vedāntic Schools 1
2. Criticism of Advaita's Avidyā by Other Thinkers 3
3. Historical Introduction 4
4. Philosophical Perspective 8
   A. Distinction between standpoints and Levels of Reality 9
   B. Distinction between two kinds of Metaphysics 14
   C. Distinction between two kinds of Scripture 16
   D. The role of Avidyā 19

Chapter Two—THE LOCUS OF AVIDYĀ

1. Introduction 25
2. Āśraya-Anupapatti 1 27
   A. Objection 1 27
   B. Reply 1 27
   C. Objection 2 28
   D. Objection 3 29
   E. Reply 2 30
   F. Objection 4 31
3. The Fallacy of Infinite Regress 32
4. Theory of Inexplicability 32
   A. Reply 3 33
      1. No reciprocal dependence 33
      2. No infinite regress 34
      3. No basic defect 34
5. Inexplicability 35
6. Āśraya-Anupapatti 2 35
   A. Objection 1 36
   B. Reply 1 36
   C. Objection 2 37
   D. Reply 2 37
   E. Objection 3 37

F. Reply 3 39
G. Objection 4 40
H. Reply 4 41
I. Objection 5 42
J. Reply 5 42
K. Objection 6 43
L. Reply 6 44

CHAPTER THREE—THE UNTENABILITY OF OBSCURATION

1. Introduction 45
A. The Jīva 46
B. Īśvara 1 46
C. Īśvara 2 47
D. Brahman 49
E. Avidyā 49
F. Adhyāsa 51
2. Rāmānuja's Tirodhāna-Anupapatti 53
A. Objection 53
B. Reply 54
C. Objection 2 55
D. Reply 2 55
E. Objection 3 56
F. Reply 3 56
G. Objection 4 56
H. Reply 4 57

CHAPTER FOUR—THE UNTENABILITY OF AVIDYĀ'S NATURE

1. Introduction 59
A. Cognizability 59
B. Objection 1 60
C. Reply 1 61
2. Rāmānuja's Svarūpa-Anupapatti 62
A. Objection 62
B. Reply 65
3. Māyā and Avidyā 66

CHAPTER FIVE—THE UNTENABILITY OF INEXPLICABILITY

1. Introduction 69
2. Rāmānuja's Anirvacanīya-Anupapatti 72
   - A. Post-Rāmānuja Objection 1 73
   - B. Reply 1 74
   - C. Objection 1a 75
   - D. Reply 1a 75
   - E. Reply 1b 75
   - F. Objection 2 76
   - G. Reply 2 76

CHAPTER SIX—IGNORANCE CANNOT BE POSITIVE

1. Introduction 79
2. Two Powers 80
3. Avidyā as the cause of the world 81
   - A. Objection 1 82
   - B. Reply 1 82
   - C. Objection 2 84
   - D. Reply 2 84
   - E. Objection 3 85
   - F. Reply 3 85
4. Terminable 86
5. Different from prior non-existence 87
6. Perception 87
   - A. Rāmānuja's objection 1 88
   - B. Reply 1 88
7. Inference 92
   - A. Rāmānuja's objection 1 93
   - B. Reply 1 94
8. Scripture 94
   - A. Rāmānuja's objection 1 95
   - B. Reply 1 96
9. Presumption 96
10. Conclusion 97

CHAPTER SEVEN—THE UNTENABILITY OF REMOVABILITY

1. Introduction 99
2. Rāmānuja's Objection 1 99
   A. Objection against perception 100
      i. Advaita's reply 101
      ii. Reply 2 102
      iii. Reply 3 103
   B. Objection against inference 104
      i. Reply 105
   C. Verbal Testimony 105
      i. Argument 1 105
      ii. Reply 106
      iii. Argument 2 106
      iv. Reply 107
   D. Objection 2 109
      i. Reply 2 109
   E. Objection 3 109
      i. Reply 3 110
   F. Argument 3 111

CHAPTER EIGHT—IGNORANCE IS NOT REMOVED BY BRAHMAN KNOWLEDGE

A. Introduction 113
B. Objection 1 114
C. Objection 2 114
D. Reply 114
E. Objection 3 116
F. Reply 118

CHAPTER NINE—CONCLUSION 119
Bibliography 125
Index 129

PREFACE

The purpose of the present study is to present an introduction to the key-concept of Advaita Vedānta, i.e. *avidyā/māyā*, along with some of the criticisms which have been levelled against this concept by Viśiṣṭādvaita Vedānta. The main exposition is an analysis of Rāmānuja's *sapta-vidhā anupapatti*, along with both historical, and possible, replies to his charges. As well, I have included subsequent objections which post-Rāmānuja followers such as Vedānta Deśika brought forth and some subsequent replies by post-Śaṅkara Advaitins.

This study stems from work which was done at the Radhakrishnan Institute for Advanced Study in Philosophy. I have endeavoured to remain faithful to both traditions—though my own philosophical predilection hints at the logical soundness of Advaita's reasoning. This is not to say, however, that all Vedāntic schools don't have a certain logic and appeal, to them. As is popularly quoted, "Vedānta is the 'crown of creation' within the Indian philosophical world".

Since I am working on a definitive work regarding the Advaita key-concept of *avidyā/māyā*, what I have attempted to do in this study is to present a basic summary of the philosophical positions of this concept from two perspectives—in a dialectical style. Rāmānuja rightly understood that in order to advance the doctrine of Viśiṣṭādvaita, he would first have to refute Advaita. Thus, his *Śrī-bhāṣya* opens with the 140 page *mahā-siddhānta* attacking the key-concept of Advaita. There are those scholars who maintain that it was not necessary to commence with, and at such great length, this refutation. However, I believe that history has confirmed his wisdom in light of the voluminous dialectical literature which now exists on just this point.

I would like to acknowledge S.M.S. Srinivasa Chari's *ADVAITA AND VIŚIṢṬĀDVAITA* which I found extremely useful as an exposition of post-Rāmānuja dialectics from the Viśiṣṭādvaita perspective. At the same time, I would like to state that my primary concern was not just a cataloging of commonly shared, and genuinely divergent, philosophical points of view between the two schools. To paraphrase Sureśvara, the main function of a dialectics is to both define, distinguish, and clarify one's own philosophical position such that it will enable one to reach the goal of life, i.e. *mokṣa*.

I studied Vedānta with Professor R. Balasubramanian at the Radhakrishnan Institute for Advanced Study in Philosophy and it is to him that I owe my knowledge of Advaita. I take this opportunity to express my gratitude to him for his help and guidance. It is impossible for me to adequately express my indebtedness to him.

I am also thankful to the Radhakrishnan Institute for offering me a place to conduct my research. Further, while it is impossible to list the names of everyone, I must not fail to acknowledge Dr. P.K. Sundaram, for his academic assistance and constant friendship.

My most recent debt is to the Department of Religious Studies, University of Lethbridge, for everything.

Finally, I would like to thank Mr. Jain and Motilal Banarsidass Publishers Pvt. Ltd., for taking the time and effort to encourage and support this publication.

Lethbridge
August 7, 1989

J. GRIMES

CHAPTER ONE

INTRODUCTION

INTRODUCTION TO THE VEDĀNTIC SCHOOLS

The word '*vedānta*' means, quite literally, the 'end of the *Veda*'. Historically, as we shall shortly observe, the concluding portion of the *Vedas* came to be called the *Upaniṣads*. By association, the philosophical schools which based their thought upon the *Upaniṣads* are also called Vedānta.

Since Upaniṣadic thought is not comprised of any consistent system and seemingly propounds different views, it became necessary to systematize it. Bādarāyaṇa (c. 400 B.C.) attempted this systematization in the form of short aphorisms called *sūtras*.[1] His work, the *Vedānta-sūtra*, is also called *Brahma-sūtra* because it is an exposition of, and enquiry into, *Brahman*. The first *sūtra* begins, *athāto brahma-jijñāsā*—now, therefore, the enquiry into the Absolute (*Brahman*).

Together with the *Dharma-sūtra* of Jaimini, which is an enquiry into the duties (*dharma*) enjoined by the *Vedas*, these two investigations (*mīmāṃsā*) form a systematic enquiry into the contents and purport of the entire *Veda*.[2]

The *Brahma-sūtras*, being pithy and Proteus-like, are unintelligible by themselves and require interpretation. Indian tradition refers to at least twenty-one different commentaries with differing shades of interpretation among them.

The reasons why the same work could give rise to so many conflicting schools of thought include: any *sūtra's* brevity leaves

1. The definition of a *sūtra* is: It must be brief; with the words not further reducible; clear; comprehensive; penetrate the essence meant; and faultless grammarwise. (*alpākṣaramasandigdhaṃ sāravad viśvatomukham/astobhamanavadyaṃ ca sūtraṃ sūtravido viduḥ//*)
2. The *Dharma-sūtra* begins, *athāto dharma-jijñāsā*. Compare this with the beginning of the *Brahma-sūtra* which begins, *athāto brahma-jijñāsā*. This is a noteworthy point for our study because Viśiṣṭādvaita claims that these two investigations form one body, while Advaita says that there is no necessary relationship between them.

much to be supplied by the commentators; without a prior philosophical tradition to rely upon, each commentator was free to follow his own ideas; since the *sūtras* do not state which Upaniṣadic text they are based upon, the individual commentators saw different topics being discussed in a given *sūtra.*

The oldest extant commentary, and easily the most famous, is by Śaṅkara (788-820 A.D.), the great exponent of Advaita Vedānta. We will also be concerned with Rāmānuja's (1017-1137 A.D.) commentary, the *Śrī-bhāṣya,* because it is there that the seven great untenables against Advaita's doctrine of *avidyā* first appeared.

Our concern in this work is with the two Vedāntic positions: Advaita and Viśiṣṭādvaita. While both schools accept the aphorism, "*Brahman* is realized as one's own *Ātman*"[3], they interpret it differently. Advaita posits a radical non-difference between *Brahman* and *Ātman,* while Viśiṣṭādvaita maintains an organic unity which preserves both unity and diversity.

The quarrels between the Advaitins and the Viśiṣṭādvaitins seem to be unending. However, it is noteworthy to remember that these disagreements are based, not on the identity of fundamental positions, but on disagreements respecting them. The special feature of Vedāntic thought is that it is a systematised exposition of accepted canonical texts. Vedāntic thought is not woven out of a particular commentator's mind so much as it is an exegesis which is grounded in, and must be true to, a given body of scriptural texts. With this in mind, one of our over-riding concerns will be to see that the concepts fundamental to each individual system are understood properly and in their true light.

Broadly speaking, the Vedānta schools may be divided into two main divisions with certain particular tendencies: (1) Non-dualistic with Absolutistic tendencies and (2) Dualistic with Theistic tendencies. Advaita Vedānta is the representative of the Non-dualistic tradition. The Theistic tradition has five major representatives: Viśiṣṭādvaita, Dvaita, Dvaitādvaita, Śuddhādvaita, and Acintyabhedābheda. These five are better known as the schools of Vaiṣṇavism.[4] As well, there are other founders of

3. *Brahma-sūtra,* IV.1.3.
4. The founders of these schools are: Rāmānuja (1017-1137 A.D.); Madhva (1199-1276 A.D.); Nimbārka (11th c.); Vallabha (1479-1531 A.D.); and Śrīcaitanya (1485-1533 A.D.).

Vedāntic schools but they are not so prominent or well-known as these.[5]

As this work is a critical study of Advaita's doctrine of *avidyā*, together with Viśiṣṭādvaita's criticisms thereon, it will be these two schools exclusively that will concern us. This is not to say that the other Vedāntic schools did not propose their own criticisms of Advaita's doctrine. It is just that Viśiṣṭādvaita's objections, especially Rāmānuja's, are so well-formulated and copious that there is very little that can be added to them.

Criticism of Advaita's Avidyā by Other Thinkers

We have noted that the Advaita doctrine was first systematically expounded by Śaṅkara. The first elaborate criticism of Advaita's doctrine of *avidyā* was given by Bhāskara (9th c. A.D.) in his commentary on the *Brahma-sūtra* called *Bhāskarabhāṣya*. He was an advocate of the Bhedābheda system of thought and regarded Advaita as but a version of Mādhyamika Buddhism.[6]

The first Viśiṣṭādvaitin who criticised *avidyā* in his *Saṃvit-siddhi* was Yāmunācārya (916-1036 A.D.). After Yāmuna came Rāmānuja and his *Śrī-bhāṣya*. Rāmānuja's arguments were further elaborated upon by Vedānta Deśika in his *Śatadūṣaṇī* and by Sudarśana in his *Śrutaprakāśikā*—both of which are commentaries on the *Śrī-bhāṣya*.

In the Twentieth Century, two Viśiṣṭādvaitins have again taken up the polemics in reply to a modern Advaitic work. These are: *Paramārthabhūṣaṇam* by Sri Uttamoor Viraraghavacharya Swami and *Tattvasudhā* by Vidwan E.S. Varadacharya. These two works were written in reply to a book entitled *Śatabhūṣaṇī* by Śri Anantakrishna Sastriar—which itself was a reply to Vedānta Deśika's *Śatadūṣaṇī*.

After Rāmānuja, Madhva (1199-1276 A.D.) is considered to be the greatest critic of Advaita. His objections are not set down in one specific place, like Rāmānuja's 'seven major objections—*saptavidhā anupapatti*', but can be found scattered throughout his

5. Viz., Bhāskara, Yādavaprakāśa, Keśava, Nīlakaṇṭha, and Baladeva.
6. Vide Srinivasachari, *The Philosophy of Bhedābheda*.

works.[7] Jayatīrtha (1365–1388 A.D.), a Dvaitin like Madhva, wrote a small independent treatise called *Vādāvalī*, which was based upon Madhva's works. In this work, Jayatīrtha criticises the Advaita doctrine of *avidyā*. Then, based upon the *Vādāvalī*, Vyāsarāya (1478–1539 A.D.) wrote his famous polemic work, *Nyāyāmṛtam*. Finally, there is Rāmācārya's *Taraṅgiṇī*, which was a reply to the criticism of the *Nyāyāmṛtam* found in the *Advaita-siddhi* of Madhusūdana Sarasvatī.

In brief, these are the major polemical works written by the major Vedāntic schools in criticism of Advaita's doctrine of *avidyā*.

In reply, some of the more famous dialectical works of Advaita include: Śrī-harṣa's *Khaṇḍana-khaṇḍa-khādya*; Citsukha's *Tattva-pradīpikā*; Ānandabodha's *Nyāyamakaranda*; Madhusūdana Sarasvatī's *Advaita-siddhi*; and Brahmānanda's *Gauḍa-brahmā-nandī*, also known as *Laghu-candrikā*. Lastly, there is Rāmarāya-kavi's *Śrī-śaṅkarāśaṅkara-bhāṣya-vimarśaḥ*, which contains a reply to the later Viśiṣṭādvaitin's objections to *avidyā*.

These works all make a significant contribution to the dialectics of Vedānta and not only help to expound the essential doctrines of the various Vedāntic schools, but also enable individuals to become clearer as to the true meaning thereof.

Historical Introduction

Source Books: Indian philosophy is generally discussed in terms of six major orthodox (*āstika*) schools and three major heterodox (*nāstika*) schools.[8] As applied in this context, 'orthodox' means an acceptance of the authority of the *Vedas* and 'heterodox' means a non-acceptance of the Vedic authority.

Orthodox Indian thought maintains that the *Vedas* constitute revelations which were neither composed nor produced by an author. Thus, the *Vedas* are said to be impersonal (*apauruṣeya*). They are referred to as *śruti* (that which is 'heard') and are

7. Vide K. Narain, *A Critique of Mādhva Refutation of the Śaṅkara School of Vedānta*.
8. Orthodox: Nyāya, Vaiśeṣika, Sāṅkhya, Yoga, Mīmāṃsā, Vedānta. Heterodox: Cārvāka, Jainism, Buddhism.

believed to be what was spontaneously heard by the Vedic seers (*ṛṣis*).

In a general sense, the *Vedas*[9] are a collection of hymns (*saṃhitā*) signifying revealed wisdom or metaphysical knowledge. More technically, each *Veda* is composed of: *Mantra*, *Brāhmaṇa*, *Āraṇyaka* and *Upaniṣad*. The *Mantras* are hymns, prayers, and sacrificial formulae; the *Brāhmaṇas* are explanatory treatises on the *Mantras* for the performance of sacrificial rites; the *Āraṇyakas* are 'forest-books' attached to the *Brāhmaṇas* which give philosophical interpretations to the latter by allegorizing them as well as prescribing various types of meditation; the *Upaniṣads* deal with knowledge of *Brahman* and make explicit what was implied in the *Mantras*.

The *Upaniṣads* form the concluding portions of the *Vedas* as arranged by Veda-vyāsa (Kṛṣṇa-Dvaipāyana), the legendary arranger or compiler of the *Vedas*. Thus, they are called '*Vedānta*' (*Veda*+*anta*: end of the *Veda*). The term is very apt for, like most Sanskrit terms, there is a *śleṣa* or rhetorical figure involved. Sanskrit roots are multi-significant or multi-valent. Besides literally expressing the fact that the *Upaniṣads* form the concluding part (*avasānabhāga*) of the *Veda*, the term also expresses the idea that the *Upaniṣads* represent the 'aim' or 'goal' of the *Veda*. Being known as the crown or summit of the *Vedas* (*śruti-śiras*), the Sanskrit word '*anta*', like the English word 'end', may be used to mean both 'terminus' and 'aim'. The aim or goal of Vedānta, both as applied to the *Upaniṣads* as well as the philosophical systems of that name, concerns the nature of *Brahman*.

In its widest sense, the term '*Vedānta*' means:

> The *Upaniṣads*, the source of right knowledge, and the *Śārīraka-sūtras*, and other treatises that help to understand their meaning (such as the *Bhagavad-gītā* and the commentaries on the *Upaniṣads*, the *Śārīraka-sūtras*, and the *Gītā*.[10]

As we observed, the Vedāntic schools derive their name of 'Vedānta' from the fact that they claim to interpret the *Upaniṣads*, as

9. There are four *Vedas*: *Ṛg Veda*, *Sāma Veda*, *Yajur Veda*, and *Atharva Veda*.
10. *Vedānta-sāra*, Section 3.

well as found their individual systems upon them. Their difference lies primarily in that the theistic traditions of Vedānta uphold a cosmic view of *Brahman* while the non-dualistic tradition propounds an acosmic view.[11]

Thus, the three basic texts of Vedānta are: the *Upaniṣads*, the *Bhagavad-gītā*, and the *Brahma-sūtras*. Together these three are known as the *prasthāna-traya*—the triple-canon of Vedānta. '*Prasthāna*' means 'foundation' and thus these three constitute the three foundations of: Revelation (*śruti*), Rememberance (*smṛti*), and Reason (*nyāya*). They are respectively known as: the *Upaniṣads* or *Śruti-prasthāna*, the *Bhagavad-gītā* or *Smṛti-prasthāna*, and the *Brahma-sūtras* or *Nyāya-prasthāna*.

Earlier we noted that the *Vedas* are referred to as *śruti* and since the *Upaniṣads* form part of the *Vedas*, their name as *Śruti-prasthāna* is apt. The *Bhagavad-gītā* stands next to the *Upaniṣads* regarding authoritativeness and is considered almost an equal. It is the immortal 'song of the divine'; Lord Kṛṣṇa's message to humanity. It forms part of the Epic, the *Mahābhārata*[12] which is a *smṛti* or remembered text. Thus it is known as the *Smṛti-prasthāna*. The *Brahma-sūtra* represents the standpoint of reason because it sets forth the Vedāntic teachings in a logical order. It is also called: *Uttara-mīmāṃsā-sūtra* since it is an enquiry into the final sections of the *Veda*; *Vedānta-sūtra* since it is the aphoristic text of Vedānta; *Śārīraka-sūtra* since it is concerned with the nature and destiny of the embodied soul; and *Bhikṣu-sūtra* since those who are most competent to study it are monks or renunciants.

Thus, we see that the basic source-book of Vedānta, and therefore its basic doctrine, is based upon *śruti* and supported by *smṛti* and reasoning.[13] In light of this, the central teaching of all three source-books will be posited to be one and the same, i.e. *Brahman*.

11. Vedānta is divided into a number of schools, the principal ones being: Advaita, Viśiṣṭādvaita and Dvaita.
12. *Mahābhārata*, *Bhīṣmaparva*, chapters 25-42.
13. In the Viśiṣṭādvaita Vedānta tradition, the Tamil hymns of the Ālvārs, the *Nālāvira-divya-prabandham*, as well as the *Vaiṣṇava Āgamas* and some of the *Purāṇas*, are considered to be as authoritative as the *prasthāna-traya*. Some of the other theistic Vedāntic schools also accept additional source-books in addition to the *prasthāna-traya* but, as these systems don't concern this study, I have ignored them.

For our purposes, since the seven major objections to the Advaitin's doctrine of *avidyā/māyā* were first put forward by Rāmānuja in his commentary on the *Brahma-sūtra*, called the *Śrī-bhāṣya*, we will be concentrating on the *Brahma-sūtra* and its commentaries by Śaṅkara and Rāmānuja. This is with regard to Vedānta's major source-books.

However, we still have to note a few works of both the post-Śaṅkara era and the successors to Rāmānuja to complete our survey of relevant literature.

Beginning with the Advaita Vedānta tradition, Śaṅkara is undoubtedly the greatest exponent and consolidator of Advaita. Because it is frequently called 'the Advaita of Śaṅkara', this leads to a misunderstanding and one is likely to assume that Śaṅkara was the founder or originator of Advaita. Such an impression is false, though, without a doubt, Śaṅkara was the greatest expounder of Advaita. In actuality, Advaita has no founder in the sense that we speak of founders of other schools, e.g., Gautama as the founder of the Nyāya school or Patañjali as the founder of the Yoga school. Advaita is as old as the *Veda* and like the *Veda*, authorless and beginningless.

However, this is not to deny that Śaṅkara, as the author of the commentaries (*bhāṣya-kāra*), gets the credit for consolidating Advaita and making clear beyond doubt the basic doctrines it expounds.

The doctrine of Advaita was further elucidated by sub-commentaries and glosses on Śaṅkara's *Bhāṣyas* and independent manuals, as well as by independent treatises. Within the Advaita tradition, three kinds of works are spoken of as providing the material, in addition to the authoritative interpretation of this material, for the school. These are: the *Sūtra*-work, the *Bhāṣya*-work, and the *Vārttika*-work. Bādarāyaṇa's *Brahma-sūtra* and Śaṅkara's *Brahma-sūtra-bhāṣya* comprise the first two limbs. Sureśvara, one of Śaṅkara's direct disciples, is the *Vārṭtikakāra* for the school.[14] As such, his status is placed alongside that of Bādarāyaṇa and Śaṅkara.

14. *Bṛhadāraṇyaka-upaniṣad-bhāṣya-vārttika; Taittirīya-upaniṣad-bhāṣya-vārttika; Pañcīkaraṇa-vārttika.* The definition of a *vārttika* is:
uktānukta-duruktādi-cintā yatra pravartate/
tam granthaṃ vārttikaṃ prāhuḥ vārttikajñā manīṣiṇaḥ//

Although all Advaitins subscribe to the doctrine of non-duality, they differ in their respective modes of expounding so. After Śaṅkara, there arose within the Advaita tradition, two 'distinct schools' or ways (*prasthāna*) to interpret his thought: The *Vivaraṇa-prasthāna* and the *Bhāmatī-prasthāna.* These two schools will significantly play a part in the rebuttal of later Viśiṣṭādvaitin criticisms.

Tradition claims that the *Bhāmatī* school has its roots in the *Brahma-siddhi* of Maṇḍana, while the *Vivaraṇa* tradition has its roots in Sureśvara's works. However, though these two schools, no doubt, differ in their interpretations of certain aspects of Advaita doctrine, it must always be remembered that these differences are of an exegetical and doctrinal nature. As far as the essentials of Advaita are concerned, the two schools are in complete agreement. Both schools are based upon, and owe allegiance and inspiration to Śaṅkara. In their attempts to clarify, elucidate, and answer post-Śaṅkara objections to the doctrine, these differences arose. And yet, to quote Sureśvara, these relative perspectives are intended only to help one to realize the inward Self.[15]

Unlike in Advaita where there is no founder of the school, the founder of Viśiṣṭādvaita is Rāmānuja (1017–1137 A.D.). As such, he is the *Bhāṣyakāra.* He interpreted Vedānta in the light of the tradition which he inherited—the theistic Vaiṣṇava cult of South India. Like Śaṅkara, he interpreted Reality as non-dual. But unlike Śaṅkara, his idea was not a distinctionless, without attributes identity, but rather a non-dual organism involving internal differentiation.

Of those who followed Rāmānuja, two are of immediate concern to us. Sudarśana Sūri, who wrote a gloss on the *Śrī-bhāṣya* called *Śrutaprakāśikā* and Vedānta Deśika, who wrote a polemical work, *Śatadūṣaṇī* both raised lengthy and striking objections to the Advaitic doctrine of *avidyā.*

Philosophical Perspective

Though Śaṅkara and Rāmānuja, as Vedāntins, take their stand

15. *Bṛhadāraṇyaka-upaniṣad-bhāṣya-vārttika,* I, iv, 402.
yayā yayā bhavetpuṃsāṃ vyutpattiḥ pratyagātmani|
sā saiva prakriyeha syāt sādhvī sā cānavasthitā.||

upon the authority of the *prasthāna-traya*, the philosophical systems which emerge out of their writings are entirely different. Using the same source material, and coming from the same culture, their views and interpretations of that material and culture differ.

Under this section, I would like to make reference to:

(1) the distinction between two standpoints—the absolute and the relative.
(2) the distinction between two kinds of metaphysics—the transcendental and the empirical.
(3) the interpretation of Scripture.
(4) the role of ignorance (*avidyā*).

Distinction Between Standpoints and Levels of Reality

The central question for *Vedānta* concerns the nature of *Brahman*. The *Brahma-sūtra*, which philosophically strings together the central concepts of the *Upaniṣads* in an ordered manner, begins: "*Athāto brahma-jijñāsā*"—Now, therefore, the enquiry into *Brahman*.[16] And this enquiry is not only intellectual, but also practical.

One's enquiry into *Brahman* asks: Is *Brahman* cosmic or acosmic? Is It the cause of the world, and if so, are both real? Is It endowed with attributes or is It attributeless? The *Upaniṣads* posit *Brahman* as both: (1) the all-inclusive ground of the universe, and (2) the reality of which the universe is but an appearance. It is the difference between these two views that made possible the subsequent divergence between the later Vedāntic schools.

To understand, let alone appreciate, any philosophical system, demands that one comprehend correctly its perspective. It is crucial that one comprehends the distinction that Advaita makes between the Absolute (*pāramārthika*) and the relative (*vyāvahārika*) points of view.[17] This distinction pervades the entire system and what is true from one point of view is not so from another. Without being absolutely clear in regard to this distinction, it is

16. *Brahma-sūtra* I.1.1.
17. Actually the Advaitin admits of three levels of reality: the apparently real (*prātībhāsika*), the empirically real (*vyāvahārika*), and the Absolutely real (*pāramārthika*)—but for our purpose here, the first two may be grouped together.

likely that one will accuse the Advaitin of inconsistencies, contradictions, and absurdities.

There are not two types of being nor two truths, but one reality, one truth, as seen from two different perspectives:

> *Brahman* is known in two forms as qualified by limiting conditions owing to the distinctions of name and form, and also as the opposite of this, i.e. as what is free from all limiting conditions whatever...thus many (*śruti*) texts show *Brahman* in two forms according as it is known from the standpoint of *vidyā* or from that of *avidyā*.[18]

This distinction allows Advaita to move freely in both levels with no contradictions.

From the empirical point of view, Advaita admits of numerous distinctions. Metaphysically, there is the problem of the One and the many. Individuals are recognised as different from one another and there exists a seeming plurality of things. Epistemologically, there is the subject-object dichotomy, as well as the problem of truth and error. Ethically, there is the problem of bondage and freedom. Yet, from the absolute point of view, there is only *Brahman*/*Ātman*—one and non-dual.[19]

Either one is involved at the relative level of duality or one realizes the non-dual *Brahman* as the truth.[20] The pluralism that is experienced at the empirical level, and with which philosophical enquiry commences, is not the final truth. Advaita admits all kinds of distinctions at the empirical level, from an empirical point of view, yet denies them from an absolute point of view.

Advaita avers that anything which is experienced is real, in some sense or other.[21] Therefore, Advaita's epistemology is realistic and posits that every cognition points to an objective reference—whether veridical or erroneous. The question becomes: Exactly how real are the things that are experienced in the empi-

18. *Brahma-sūtra-bhāṣya*, I.1.11.
19. *Chāndogya Upaniṣad* 6.2.1. *ekam eva advitīyam.*
20. Ibid. 7.2.1. "...I know merely the texts, not the Self."
21. *Vedānta-paribhāṣā*, p. 7. "Just as the notion of one's identity with the body is assumed to be valid knowledge exactly so is this ordinary knowledge—till the Self is truly known."

rical world? Advaita replies that the things of the empirical world are real so long as the empirical order lasts:

> The division of real and unreal depends upon knowledge or experience: that is real whose knowledge does not miscarry; the unreal on the contrary, is the object of a knowledge which fails or goes astray.[22]

Thus, according to Śaṅkara, the real is that which lasts, which suffers no contradictions, and which is eternal and unsublatable. Things of the world may be said to be real until they suffer sublation. Thus they are called 'what is other than the real or the unreal' (*sadasad-vilakṣaṇa*), illusory (*mithyā*) and indescribable (*anirvacanīya*). Since they are cognized, they are not unreal (*asat*). Since they are sublated, they are not real (*sat*). By this criterion, *Brahman* alone is the absolutely real; never being subject to contradiction. All else can be called 'real' only by courtesy. The distinction between one individual and another, the existence of a plurality of things, the attribution of attributes to the Absolute are all concessions to the Truth made from the relative point of view.

However, to bring out the full implications of the term '*advaita*', it should be noted that such expressions as 'absolutely real' and from an 'absolute point of view' are merely contextual.[23] They are used only by way of contrast with all that is not real. In no other sense can *Brahman/Ātman* be called real. If one accepts the empirical world of plurality, then such expressions are meaningful. But to one who has realized the Truth, these expressions lose their significance. For such a one, "*Veda* is no longer *Veda*."[24]

The term '*advaita*' refers to non-duality. According to Advaita, non-duality is the Truth. And the 'non' of the expression applies not only to duality, but also to all systems. Strictly speaking, Advaita is not a system or school of philosophy. Advaita stands for the plenary experience of non-duality—the experience of Truth itself. It is ultimately not so much a theory as an experience.

22. *Bhagavad-gītā-bhāṣya* of Śaṅkara, II.16. Also see his *Brahmā-sūtra-bhāṣya* 2.1.11 and 3.2.4.
23. *Māṇḍūkya-kārika* iv.74. *ajaḥ kalpitasaṃvṛtyā paramārthena nāpi ajaḥ.*
24. *Bṛhadāraṇyaka Upaniṣad* 4.3.22. *yatra vedā avedāḥ.*

The consequences of this 'distinction between standpoints' is simple to state and devastating in its implications. At the Absolute level, '*Ātman* is *Brahman*'.

> Where verily there is, as it were, a duality, there one knows another. But when to the Knower of *Brahman*, everything has become the Self, what should one know and through what? Through what should one know That owing to which all this is known—through what, O Maitreyi, should one know the Knower?[25]

Advaita is often spoken of as a type of monism. However, Advaita or non-dualism is not a monism. Advaita emphasises 'non'; it negates all duality and difference. Differences are said to be of three kinds: internal, between members of the same class, or between different species.[26] A mere monism may not allow the latter two types of difference, but it is certainly compatible with the first type. Advaita, however, rejects all three types of difference. For this very reason, Advaitins also reject a view of the ultimate Reality as a Person (as is advocated by Theism and other monisms).

Viśiṣṭādvaita makes no such distinction between standpoints or levels of reality. Since it holds that whatever is experienced is real, there is no reason to make such a distinction.[27] Advaita makes 'eternality' the definitive of the real which means that the eternal *alone* is real. Viśiṣṭādvaita also posits that eternality is a characteristic of *Brahman*. However, Viśiṣṭādvaita amends its definition of what is real so as to accord a status of reality to the non-eternal world also.

It is true that Viśiṣṭādvaita does not claim that the reality of *Brahman* and the non-eternal world is identical. For, according to them, only the eternal *Brahman* is the independent reality. The non-eternal world is a reality dependent upon *Brahman*.

The implications of this include: while Advaita views the world as an appearance of *Brahman*, Viśiṣṭādvaita views it as a dependent reality on *Brahman*. Advaita's 'appearance' is ultimately

25. Ibid. 2.4.14.
26. *Svagata, sajātīya and vijātīya.*
27. *Yathārtham sarva-vijñānam iti veda-vidām matam.* 'All knowledge is true, so say the knowers of *Veda*.'

sublated which makes it ontologically illusory. This is consistent with Advaita's commitment to a non-relational *Brahman*.

Though Viśiṣṭādvaita's 'dependence' may seem similar to Advaita's 'appearance', it is radically different. Because they believe that a world which is admitted to be real in common experience can never be said to be illusory, from any standpoint, the non-eternal world must necessarily be dependent upon the eternal *Brahman*.

Viśiṣṭādvaita accepts three ultimate realities: God (*Īśvara*), soul (*cit*), and matter (*acit*). God alone is independent and the other two are dependent upon Him. The world of *cit* and *acit* is conceived of as the body of the Lord. It is in this connection that the key-concept of the system is formulated: *apṛthak-siddhi* or the internal relation of inseparability. The inseparable unity of God, souls and matter, with the latter two being entirely dependent upon the former, comprises Viśiṣṭādvaita's *Brahman*.

Thus, a statement like '*ekam eva advitīyam*', which the Advaitin interprets as proclaiming a non-dual *Brahman* and an illusory world, to the Viśiṣṭādvaitin implies the independence and supremacy of *Brahman* together with the world as a dependent reality. Rāmānuja admits differentiation but rejects separateness; admits distinctions and distinguishability but rejects opposition and divisibility. God, as qualified (*viśiṣṭa*) by souls and matter is non-dual (*advaita*) and hence the system is called '*Viśiṣṭa-advaita*'.

Advaita contends that the real, *Brahman*, must be unsublatable, unchanging, and therefore, it follows that the changing world must be unreal or illusory. Viśiṣṭādvaita is just as intent as Advaita in maintaining that *Brahman* is changeless. However, Viśiṣṭādvaitins must take a different course, especially since they maintain that *Brahman* is both the material cause (*upādāna-kāraṇa*) as well as the efficient cause (*nimitta-kāraṇa*) of the world.[28] They attempt this by maintaining that the plurality of the world is 'internal' to *Brahman* and that all change belongs only to the 'body', *cit* and *acit*, of *Brahman* and not to *Brahman* Itself, Which is their unchanging essence. Put into technical jargon, Viśiṣṭādvaitins maintain a distinction between the form (*svarūpa*) and the essence (*svabhāva*) of *Brahman*.

28. *Śrī-bhāṣya* I.1.1.

Another side of the consequence of this 'distinction between levels of reality' arises in regard to the 'infiniteness' of *Brahman.* The Upaniṣadic statement, "All this is only *Brahman*", *sarvaṃ khalvidaṃ brahma,*[29] surely indicates by the word 'all' (*sarvaṃ*), the plurality of the empirical world. The question naturally arises: How can the many be one?

Advaita has no trouble with this statement simply because it 'dissolves' the many from Advaita's own absolute (*pāramārthika*) level of Reality—the consequence of which places *Brahman* alone as the sole Reality.[30]

Viśiṣṭādvaita, on the other hand, is adamant about maintaining the reality of the empirical world—even from the standpoint of *Brahman.* Having accepted *Brahman* as the material cause of the world and the world as a part of *Brahman, Brahman* obviously cannot be a bare oneness, a non-dual unqualified infiniteness devoid of distinctions. Viśiṣṭādvaita wants to maintain, not only a reality possessing infinite auspicious qualities, but also an integral unity which unifies the empirical plurality with the transcendent without, at the same time, depriving them of their individuality.

Distinction Between Two Kinds of Metaphysics

Advaita begins its philosophical enquiry, here and now. Its metaphysics is immanent and empirical and not transcendental. *Brahman* is involved in, and is the basis of, all one's experiences. This is a key-point because it has several far-reaching consequences. Advaita is primarily and foremost an enquiry into *Brahman*—a *Brahman* Which is intimately and immediately involved in the individual's experiences. However, though *Brahman* is seemingly enmeshed in one's experiences, It is not consciously present to one's consciousness as the things of the empirical world are. The individual must make an earnest enquiry and divine *Brahman* through discrimination. Though *Brahman* is not something to be gained afresh; It does need to be discriminated from the not-self. This search is not divorced from experience nor is it outside

29. *Chāndogya Upaniṣad*, III.14.1.
30. *Brahma-sūtra-bhāṣya*, II.1.27; II.1.31.

of one's daily experience. It comes through an analysis of one's day-to-day experiences, at all levels.

For the Advaitin, this means that pursuit of the reality is to be done right where one is, here and now. One does not have to search for the reality elsewhere. The very depths of one's being, the Being of all beings, the Advaitin avers, is the most empirical of all.

Viśiṣṭādvaita's metaphysical view regarding *Brahman* is basically transcendental. However, it is not that of a merely transcendental Absolute existing above and beyond the finite universe. God (*Īśvara*) is both the transcendent and the immanent ground of the world. God, Whom the Viśiṣṭādvaitins identify with *Viṣṇu-Nārāyaṇa*, is the same as the Upaniṣadic *Brahman* endowed with the eternal attributes of truth, goodness, beauty, and bliss.

The Advaitins declare that when the *Upaniṣads* state that *Brahman* is *nirguṇa*, it means that It is attributeless. But, according to the Viśiṣṭādvaitins, *nirguṇa* means that God is not devoid of all attributes, but only of those attributes which are undesirable, evil and despicable. God is not a distinctionless Being, for He has internal distinctions.

According to Viśiṣṭādvaita, *Brahman* appears in five forms: (1) *Para* or His transcendent form which possesses the six attributes of lordship, potency, strength, virility, knowledge, and splendour. (2) *Vyūha* or His cosmic manifestations as Saṅkaraṣaṇa, Vāsudeva, Pradyumna, and Aniruddha. (3) *Vibhava* or His divine incarnations (*avatāras*). (4) *Antaryāmin* or the immanent form of God as the inner ruler of all. (5) *Arcā* or God in the shape of sacred idols.[31]

Though the Viśiṣṭādvaitin's *Brahman* is not merely an impassive God Who looks down upon humanity from a transcendent seat in heaven, but Who also participates in the individual's experiences of life, still, the over-riding emphasis is on a *Brahman* Who is supremely independent and ultimately transcendent *Brahman* cannot be said to suffer change for that goes against the prevailing teachings of the *Upaniṣads*. Thus, Rāmānuja had to find a way to explain how *Brahman*/*Īśvara* does not suffer change in Himself, even as the entities which comprise His body do. This is not easy

31. *Yatīndramatadīpikā*, IX.17, p. 133. *evamprakāra īśvaraḥ paravyūhavibhavāntaryāmyarcāvatārarūpeṇa pañcaprakāraḥ.*

to understand—how inseparable attributes undergo change while the constituting principle does not. Thus, *Īśvara* becomes a transcendent Absolute as well as an indwelling manifestation.

Viśiṣṭādvaita admits of several real and ultimate entities while at the same time stating that there is only one Being (which all the attribute elements derive their being from). Philosophically speaking, it is over this lack of independence which led the Advaitin to deny reality to diversity. Without pursuing this too deeply here, it would seem as though one of two consequences necessarily follows. Either diversity is real in which case the absoluteness of the Absolute falls, or else difference-in-identity is affirmed—a position which Viśiṣṭādvaita is also loath to accept.

The Distinction Between Two Kinds of Scripture

It is commonly noted that the *Upaniṣads* contain two distinct types of thought. One is an absolute idealism which Advaita seized upon to propound their doctrine that *Brahman* is the sole reality; the world is unreal; and the individual soul is non-different from *Brahman*.[32]

There is another stream of thought in the *Upaniṣads* which posits that *Brahman* is full of attributes and virtues; individual souls are real and many; and the world of name and form is real. This is the theistic approach.

These two types of Upaniṣadic passages are known as: *bheda* and *abheda* texts.

> He is Brahmā; He is Indra; He is Prajāpati; He is all these Gods; and these five great elements...[33]
>
> As Being alone was this in the beginning, one only, without a second.[34]

Advaita declares the *abheda* texts as primary and all other texts as secondary. Viśiṣṭādvaita reconciles these two streams of thought with the help of what are known as reconciliatory (*Ghaṭaka*) texts. For instance, in the passage:

32. *Brahma satyam jaganmithyā jīvo brahmaiva nā 'paraḥ.*
33. *Aitareya Upaniṣad*, V.3.
34. *Chāndogya Upaniṣad*, VI.2.1.

> He who stands on the Earth, Who is inside the Earth and Whom the Earth does not know; Whose body Earth is, and Who controls the Earth from within; He, verily, is your indwelling eternal self.[35]

This passage goes on to enumerate twenty-two objects as the body of *Brahman* of which He is the inner controller and self. It is with such reconciliatory passages that Viśiṣṭādvaita was able to equally accept the two distinct streams of thought in the *Upaniṣads*, as well as to formulate its key concept of internal inseparability between God, individual souls and the world.

A second distinction between types of Scripture involves what are called: Action-oriented texts (*karma-kāṇḍa*) and knowledge-oriented texts (*jñāna-kāṇḍa*). It is well-known that the Pūrva-mīmāṃsā philosophical tradition advocates that the entire *Veda* has ritual action (*karma*) for its purport.[36] As the ritual sections of the *Veda* occur earlier (*pūrva*) than the knowledge sections (the *Upaniṣads*), the philosophical system which is based on the earlier sections is known as Pūrva-mīmāṃsā while the philosophical traditions which are inspired by the later sections, the *Upaniṣads*, are known as Uttara-mīmāṃsā. Since Uttara-mīmāṃsā is better known by its name of 'Vedānta', Pūrva-mīmāṃsā is generally known as simply Mīmāṃsā.

Viśiṣṭādvaita maintains that the two '*mīmāṃsās*' are one body of Scripture (*ekaśāstra*). They give equal authority to each type of scriptural emphasis, i.e. action and knowledge. Scripture is a single body containing no internal stratification in terms of authenticity. There is neither a higher or a lower *Brahman*, nor a higher or lower knowledge.

Advaita, on the other hand, claims that *karma-kāṇḍa* and *jñāna-kāṇḍa* are two different bodies of Scripture and gives pride of place to Vedānta or knowledge-oriented texts. In fact, they go so far as to declare that it is knowledge of the Upaniṣadic teaching about *Brahman* alone which will lead to the final goal of liberation.

The knowledge and action oriented sections of the *Veda* seem

35. *Bṛhadāraṇyaka Upaniṣad*, V.7.22.
36. *Mīmāṃsā-sūtra* I.1.1.—*athāto dharma-jijñāsā.*

to contradict each other in what they teach. Since both sections are scriptural, it becomes necessary for each school to reconcile their mutual relation. Advaita calls them antithetical and surmounts the antithesis by stating that the two sections are addressed to two different classes of individuals.[37] The *jñāna-kāṇḍa* is intended for individuals striving to transcend ignorance while the *karma-kāṇḍa* is intended for individuals who are still under the spell of ignorance (*avidyā*). What is true and desirable from a lower point of view differs from what is true and desirable from a higher perspective.

Advaita maintains that not only is there no cause and effect relationship between knowledge and action, but also there is not even a chronological sequence there. The agent is different, i.e. the eligible person to perform action has certain requirements and is interested in ends, while the eligible person seeking knowledge has other prerequisites and is interested in liberation. The subject-matter is different, i.e. one is concerned with knowledge while the other one is concerned with action. Finally, their results are different, i.e. one gives liberation while the other gives enjoyment.

Viśiṣṭādvaita does not subscribe to this antithesis. It claims that the *Veda* is a single body of teaching intended for the same class of individuals. The two sections are complementary with the *jñāna-kāṇḍa* dwelling on the nature of God and the *karma-kāṇḍa* delineating the modes of worshipping Him.[38]

This is important because, Viśiṣṭādvaita, unlike Advaita, lays down action as a precondition into the enquiry into *Brahman*. Not only must the individual perform the actions appropriate to one's station in life throughout one's lifetime, but one may take up the study of knowledge only after imbibing the nature, limitations, and value of action.

The practice of disinterested action results in the purification of the mind. With a purified mind, the individual is qualified to seek knowledge. Knowledge is not wisdom of the Self, as in Advaita, but knowledge that the individual is dependent upon God. This paves the way for devotion which is an intense love of God and leads to liberation.

37. *Brahma-sūtra-bhāṣya*, I.1.1.
38. *Yatīndramatadīpikā*, III.6, p. 41.

THE ROLE OF AVIDYĀ

Not only is ignorance (*avidyā*) the cornerstone of this book, but it is also the cornerstone of the Advaita system. The cornerstone of any philosophical system is that 'key-concept' upon which the system revolves. For example, to sustain the radical pluralistic realism of the Vaiśeṣika school, the importance of its key-concept of inherence (*samavāya*) cannot be exaggerated. Likewise, the importance of the internal relation of inseparability (*apṛthak-siddhi*) makes it the key-concept of Viśiṣṭādvaita Vedānta. Or, to mention but a few examples from Western philosophy, Plato's concept of Form or Idea (*eidos*), Leibniz's *monad* and Bergson's *élan vital* serve as the key-concepts in their respective systems of thought.

The key-concept of Advaita Vedānta is *avidyā/māyā*.[39] This entails a little elaboration in order that a familiar misunderstanding may not result. Critics sometimes label Advaita Vedānta as '*māyā-vāda*' and Advaitins are called '*māyā-vādins*'. These terms are used disparagingly and yet there is a grain of truth in the matter. *Avidyā/māyā* cannot exist or function independent of *Brahman* and it ceases to be when *Brahman* is realized. Still, *avidyā/māyā* is the device by which the Advaitin explains how the One non-dual Reality (*Brahman*) appears as multitudinous. Strictly speaking, *Brahman* is the be-all and end-all of Advaita, and if anything, Advaita should be called '*Brahma-vāda*'. This is so because Advaita never loses sight of its central doctrine that *Brahman* is real, the world is unreal, and the individual is non-different from *Brahman*. *Avidyā* cannot function without *Brahman/jīva* as its locus and it ceases to be once realization comes. And yet, the concept of *avidyā/māyā* may still be said to be cardinal to Advaita.

What the critics have done is to mistake the means for the end. The reality of *Brahman* is Advaita's sole concern. The Advaitin is not interested in proving the existence of *avidyā/māyā*. Nonetheless, though *avidyā/māyā* is not ultimately real, its importance cannot be exaggerated for the role that it plays within Advaita.

39. Vide Radhakrishnan, *Indian Philosophy*, vol. II, p. 565; R. Balasubramanian in *Perspectives of Theism and Absolutism in Indian Philosophy*, p. 48.

The entire philosophical system of Advaita may be said to be based upon its key-concept of *avidyā*, which is also known as *māyā*.[40]

> *Ātman*, the self-luminous, though the owner of his own *Māyā*, imagines in himself, by himself (all the objects that the subject experiences within or without).[41]
>
> This unborn (changeless, non-dual *Brahman*) appears to undergo modification only on account of *Māyā* (illusion) and not otherwise.[42]

It is by means of this concept of *avidyā* that Advaita delineates its epistemology, metaphysics and practical teachings. For instance, epistemology presupposes a subject who knows, the object which is known and the resulting knowledge. The justification and elucidation of this triple form (*tripuṭī*) is accounted for by *avidyā*. Similarly with its doctrine of error, *avidyā* is error's material cause.[43] Superimposition (*adhyāsa*) and the theory of appearance (*vivartavāda*), which both help to explain the problem of error, presuppose *avidyā*. An inert, material mind needs the help of consciousness for knowledge to arise. Knowledge exists in and through a conscious experience of multiplicity. And it is *avidyā* which is the cause of all these empirical distinctions. The Advaitin contends that the very possibility of empirical distinctions rests upon the existence of *avidyā*.

According to the metaphysics of Advaita, the Absolute (*Brahman*) is One and non-dual. It is undifferentiated, non-relational, non-dual consciousness appearing in the two forms of God (*Īśvara*) and individuals (*jīva*) due to *avidyā*. Thus arises the apparent problem of the One and the many. What is the relation-

40. Vide Śaṅkara's commentaries on the *Kaṭha Upaniṣad* III.11 and the *Brahma-sūtra* I.4.3, wherein he says that the root-cause of the world is *māyā* as *avidyā*. Some post-Śaṅkara Advaitins draw a distinction between them, i.e. Bhāratītīrtha on the grounds that *māyā* is rooted in *Īśvara* and *avidyā* in *jīva*.
41. *Māṇḍūkyopaniṣad* with Gauḍapāda's *Kārikā* and Śaṅkara's *Commentary*, II.12, p. 97. *kalpayati ātmanā ātmānam ātmā devaḥ svamāyayā.*
42. Ibid., III.19, p. 166. *māyayā bhidyate hi etat na anyathā ajam kathañcana.*
43. T.M.P. Mahadevan, *The Philosophy of Advaita*, p. 79.

ship between the One and the many, between the Absolute and the relative? The Advaitin must account for the seeming plurality of the universe if the Reality is One and non-dual. An explanation is also called for in regard to the distinction which the Advaitin makes between the Reality with form (*saguṇa*) and the formless Reality (*nirguṇa Brahman*). The seeming difference between the individual soul and the Absolute needs to be explained. The place of *Īśvara*, as well as the creation of the world, must be accounted for. Every metaphysical system endeavours to explain these three entities, i.e. the Reality, the individual self and the physical universe. Advaita must explain how these three entities are really only one. And this, Advaita does, by elucidating how the concept of *avidyā* is presupposed in each of these issues.

Lastly, the entire practical teachings of Advaita presuppose the concept of *avidyā*. The bondage of the individual, as well as the individual's liberation, hinges upon *avidyā*. *Avidyā* is the root cause of bondage and knowledge is the direct means of its removal. Ethics, aesthetics and values all have meaning only within the context of *avidyā*. Likewise, all disciplines prescribed for attaining release only become meaningful within the context of *avidyā*.

According to the Advaitin, *avidyā* has six aspects: (1) it is beginningless (*anādi*); (2) it can be terminated by knowledge (*jñāna-nivartya*); (3) it is a positive entity (*bhāva-rūpa*); (4) its ontological status is neither real nor unreal (*anirvacanīya*); (5) it has the two powers of concealment and projection (*āvaraṇa* and *vikṣepa-śakti*); (6) its locus (*āśraya*) is either *Brahman* or *jīva*.

According to Viśiṣṭādvaita, Advaita's theory of *avidyā* does not satisfactorily solve any of these philosophical problems. Instead it merely explains away these problems. Thus, this doctrine of *avidyā* became the main target of criticism by Viśiṣṭādvaitins. Proof of this is the fact that Rāmānuja begins his *Śrī-bhāṣya* with the *mahāpūrvapakṣa* of the Advaitin's position on *avidyā* and then proceeds to spend considerable space, time and energy to refute it.

Many critics of Rāmānuja have wondered why he spent so much time over a rebuttal of Advaita's *avidyā*.[44] To Rāmānuja's

44. *Śrī-bhāṣya*, I.1.1. The *pūrva-pakṣa* takes up most of the first *sūtra's* commentary.

genius, he recognized that he could not erect a sound philosophy that would endure without first removing the predominant existing system. He further recognized that the key-concept that ties together all of Advaita's thought is *avidyā*—thus his *mahā-siddhānta*.

Rāmānuja states: (1) the very nature (*svarūpa*) of *avidyā* is riddled with contradictions; (2) its description as inexplicable (*anirvacanīya*) is untenable; (3) no valid means of knowledge (*pramāṇa*) supports such a theory; (4) the locus (*āśraya*) of *avidyā* can be neither *Brahman* nor *jīva*; (5) it is unintelligible to claim that *avidyā* can obscure (*tirodhāna*) the nature of *Brahman*; (6) its removal by right knowledge (*jñāna-nivartya*) is untenable; (7) the very conception of the cessation of *avidyā* (*avidyā-nivṛtti*) is absurd. This is the sevenfold criticism (*sapta-vidhā anupapatti*) levelled against the Advaitin's doctrine of *avidyā* by Rāmānuja.

The key-concept in Advaita is *avidyā/māyā*. Though *māyā* is admitted by the other schools, it is understood differently. *Īśvara* has been described as a magician (*Māyāvī*) in the *Upaniṣads*[45] and *māyā* as the wonderful power which *Īśvara* wields. In evoking these references, Rāmānuja contends that: *māyā* is real; the objects created by God employing this power are real; *māyā* itself has only the power of projection (*vikṣepa*) or change (*pariṇāma*). The transformation of *māyā* is determined by God, according to Viśiṣṭādvaita, while it takes place of its own accord, according to Sāṅkhya.

Advaitins contend that: *māyā* is neither real nor unreal; the universe of multiplicity is ultimately unreal; *māyā* has both the power of concealment as well as of projection; *Brahman* is the material cause of the universe (as *māyā*) as appearance (*vivarto-pādāna*) and not as transformation (*pariṇāma*).

All Vedāntins accept that *māyā* has the power of projection. What distinguishes Advaita from the others is that it holds that *māyā* also has the power of concealment. Their theory that the universe is but a mere appearance, and not a transformation, of *Brahman* hinges upon this distinction. As well, it explains how, even with the disappearance of concealment (*māyā ipso facto*

45. Vide *Ṛg Veda* VI.47.18; *Śvetāśvatara Upaniṣad* 4.10; *Bhagavad-gītā* IV.5-7 and XVIII.61. Vide also *Ṛg Veda* I.159.4; III.38.7; V.85.5; IX.83.3.

disappearing) through residual latent impressions, projection may still persist—a fact borne out by *jīvanmuktas* (those liberated even while living in a human body).

Finally, much of the criticism of Advaita's doctrine of *avidyā/māyā* is due to the critics mistaking it for illusoriness or non-existence. The Advaitin contends that the universe of multiplicity is *mithyā*, neither real nor unreal—but not *asat*—unreal. This point is extremely important to understand it correctly. Much confusion has arisen precisely because it hasn't been properly understood. Because the world appears, it is said to be 'not unreal'. But because the world is ultimately sublatable, it is said to be 'not real'.

The critics have pondered, 'why not call it both real and unreal?' This is unacceptable to the Advaitins because what is real by definition can never change or be sublated and because what is unreal can never appear as an existent.

Advaitins contend that the world is false, not to those individuals who experience the world, but only to liberated individuals. It is from a *jīvanmukta's* standpoint that the 'falseness' of the world is asserted, and not from that of an individual who is in the world and of the world. The level of reality and perspective is all-important.

Chapter Two

THE LOCUS OF AVIDYĀ

Introduction

Śaṅkara stated, "*Avidyā* is *parameśvarāśrayā*, that is, it depends upon *Brahman*. And in it (*avidyā*) the *jīvas*, having lost their identity with *Brahman*, rest."[1] All Advaitins subscribe to the position that *Brahman* is attributeless (*nirguṇa*), undifferentiated (*nirviśeṣa*), One and non-dual and that the universe of multiplicity appears due to ignorance (*avidyā*). The question is, 'Where is the locus of *avidyā*? Where does it stand and what is its content?' If *Brahman* is really *nirguṇa* and *nirviśeṣa*, then there is no place for *avidyā* to be located.

Avidyā implies some entity it belongs to and some object to which it refers. Both Advaitins and critics of Advaita are divided over this question. The Bhāmatī school maintains that the individual (*jīva*) is the locus of *avidyā*, while the Vivaraṇa school holds that *Brahman* is the locus of *avidyā*.[2]

All Advaitins are in agreement that the content of *avidyā* is *Brahman*. The nature of *avidyā* is to conceal something and concealment is possible only with reference to a self-luminous entity. As everything except *Brahman* is inert and insentient, it needs no external cause for being concealed. Thus, *Brahman* alone is capable of being concealed (and therefore the content of *avidyā*). This will be dealt with further in the chapter regarding the obscuration of *avidyā*.

Critics of Advaita are of the opinion that both the theory that the *jīva* is the locus of *avidyā* (*jīva-ajñāna-vāda*) and the theory

1. *Brahma-sūtra-bhāṣya*, I.4.3. *avidyātmikā hi bījaśaktiḥ avyaktaśabdanirdeśyā māyāmayī mahāsuṣuptiḥ, yasyāṃ śerate svarūpapratibodharahitāḥ saṃsāriṇo jīvāḥ*; *Bṛhadāraṇyakopaniṣad-bhāṣya* III.viii.12; *Bhagavad-gītā-bhāṣya* XIII.2.
2. Bhāmatī school: Maṇḍana's *Brahma-siddhi* Part I, p. 10; Vācaspati's *Bhāmatī*, p. 297. Vivaraṇa school: Sureśvara's *Naiṣkarmya-siddhi*, Ch. II and *Bṛhadāraṇyaka-upaniṣad-bhāṣya-vārttika* I.iv.1215–1227; Sarvajñātman's *Saṃkṣepaśārīraka* I.319 and III.15.

that *Brahman* is the locus of *avidyā* (*brahma-ajñāna-vāda*) are untenable. In this regard, the criticisms of Rāmānuja, Sudarśana and Vedānta Deśika will be juxtaposed with the dialectics of the post-Śaṅkara Advaitins.

A distinctive feature of Indian philosophy is the manner in which each school conducts a systematic exposition of its doctrine. The method of exposition adopted by each philosopher is to establish his own position through a progressive criticism of the rival views. These rival views are called the *pūrva-pakṣa.* They are examined in sequence, beginning with the least acceptable view followed by each subsequent view being criticized in light of the prior objection. Finally, when even the most proximate view is rejected, the philosopher's own standpoint or settled conclusion (*siddhānta*) is established. Thus, in every philosophical classic, there is a dialectical movement towards the author's final position through a progressive criticism of other perspectives.

Rāmānuja, in his *Śrī-bhāṣya*, begins with a minor objection (*laghu-pūrva-pakṣa*) and a minor reply (*laghu-siddhānta*) before he launches into his seven major objections to the Advaitin's doctrine of *avidyā.* Then comes the great rival view (the famous *mahā-pūrva-pakṣa* of Rāmānuja) and the great conclusion (*mahā-siddhānta*).

To Rāmānuja's credit, notice how beautifully and accurately he describes the Advaitin's position:

> *Brahman*, the non-differentiated Consciousness, is the only reality, and all this manifoldness is imagined in It alone and is false. Due to the effect of beginningless Nescience which is unspeakable, this manifoldness is wrongly imagined in the one non-dual *Brahman* Which is pure Consciousness.[3]

Rāmānuja continues at great length to describe the Advaitin's position before he begins to refute it. Then he launches into nine lengthy objections before arriving at the first untenable—the untenability of *jīva*/*Brahman* as a locus of *avidyā* (*āśraya-anupapatti*).

3. *Śrī-bhāṣya*, I.1.1, pp. 8-9.

ĀŚRAYA-ANUPAPATTI—1

Objection 1

The Bhāmatī view declares that the *jīva* is the locus of *avidyā*. This position is so incredulous to Rāmānuja that he dismisses it in one sentence. He says, "It cannot be the former for the individual soul (*jīva*) comes into existence only after *Brahman* is covered by ignorance."[4]

Rāmānuja's objection claims that the fallacy of reciprocal dependence (*anyo'nyāśraya*) is involved if one posits that the *jīva* is the locus of *avidyā*. *Avidyā* presupposes the appearance of the *jīva* and simultaneously, the *jīva* is the result of *avidyā*.

Reply 1

According to Maṇḍana, there are two ways in which this objection can be met. First, even though the *jīva* and *avidyā* are both said to be beginningless, one does not precede the other in time. He employs an analogy of the seed and sprout series to elucidate the idea that there is no chronological priority for either member of the series. As well, one could ask, 'Which came first, the chicken or the egg?' We know that there are *avidyā*, *jīvas*, chickens, eggs, seeds and sprouts, and to ask which came first is meaningless and irrelevant.

The other way that Maṇḍana meets this objection is to categorically state that, by definition, *avidyā* does not admit of a logical, cogent analysis. Maṇḍana says,

> In *avidyā-māyā* there is nothing which is inconsistent, improbable, illegitimate. If it conveys what is consistent and congruous, it ceases to be *māyā*.[5]

If this were the case, then *avidyā* would cease to be *avidyā*! What is true of the things of the world is not, and need not be, true of *avidyā*. Objects of the world must necessarily follow a causal sequence such that the effect can never be the cause of its

4. Ibid., p. 55.
5. *Brahma-siddhi* Part I, p. 10. *na hi māyāyāṃ kācidanupapattiḥ; anupapadyamānārthaiva hi māyā; upapadyamānārthatvayathārthabhāvānna māyā syāt.*

cause. But *avidyā* is a riddle. Unintelligibility itself is the characteristic feature of it. "Wonder is its garments; inscrutable is its nature."[6]

It should also be noted here that it is no argument to say that the *jīva* cannot be the locus of *avidyā* on the ground that the *jīva* is non-different from *Brahman*. This would be a misinterpretation of the Advaitin's doctrine. The *jīva* is non-different from *Brahman* only from an absolute perspective. When the *jīva* is associated with the adjunct of *avidyā*, it is seemingly different from *Brahman*.

Objection 2

The Vivaraṇa school also calls the theory that the *jīva* is the locus of *avidyā* untenable. As a side-objection, Sarvajñātman points out that *avidyā* presupposes the appearance of the *jīva* and hence cannot be its locus.[7] Even if it is accepted that both the *jīva* and *avidyā* are beginningless, still, this distinction can only be made from the perspective of multiplicity. The idea of a *jīva* does not arise if one has realized *Brahman*. Thus, it follows that the *jīva* derives its existence from *avidyā*—even if *avidyā* does not necessarily require the notion of the *jīva* for its own existence. This relation is not one of cause and effect. To put it in philosophical jargon, it is a mode of the pervader and the pervaded (*vyāpya-vyāpaka-bhāva*).

A second objection put forward by Sarvajñātman concerns the fact that the *jīva* is what is technically called 'a blend of *Brahman* and the internal organ'. This has the consequence of establishing *avidyā* in itself, which is an impossibility. If *avidyā* is said to have its locus in the *jīva*, and the *jīva* is, by definition, a blend of *Brahman* plus the internal organ, then it means that *avidyā* is present in *Brahman* and the internal organ. With the internal organ being known to be an effect of *avidyā* (and as such, of the nature of *avidyā*), it follows that *avidyā* resides in itself, which is impossible.

A third objection raised by Sarvajñātman hinges upon an analysis of the deep sleep state. In the deep sleep state there is an

6. *Pañcadaśī* VI.139. *vismayaikaśarīrāyā māyāyāścodyarūpataḥ.*

7. *Saṃkṣepaśārīraka* II.209. *ajñānātmakavastu nāśrayatayājñānasya saṃbhāvyate.*

experience of *avidyā*. This is borne out by the testimony of a person who, upon waking, says: 'I did not know anything when I was asleep.' The person was enveloped in *avidyā*, and acknowledges its presence even while asleep (i.e. 'I did not know anything'), even though there is an absence of the notion of *jīva*-hood. If *avidyā* can be directly experienced in the absence of the *jīva*, this proves that the *jīva* cannot be the locus of *avidyā*.

Such objections have led the Vivaraṇa school to say that pure Consciousness (*Brahman*) must be the locus of *avidyā*. In the deep sleep state, only pure Consciousness and *avidyā* exist. An individual would not be able to experience *avidyā* if *avidyā* did not have a locus. Thus, it must be deduced that pure Consciousness or *Brahman* is its locus.

Objection 3

The view that the individual self is the locus of *avidyā* is inadmissible according to Vedānta Deśika. The Bhāmatī school has contended that *Brahman* is not directly associated with *avidyā*, but is reflected in the *jīva*. Thus *Brahman* (the reflection) is unaffected by any defects found in the *jīva* (the prototype), even as the defects of a mirror found in the reflection of a face, do not belong to the face.

Vedānta Deśika refutes this theory. He commences by noting that a reflection of consciousness in the inner organ (or *avidyā*) is an impossibility. Reflections, he claims, can only occur of entities which possess physical attributes. Both the object reflected and the reflecting medium must possess colour and form. But neither *avidyā* nor pure Consciousness possesses such features.

His second objection grants, for the sake of argument, that perhaps a reflection is somehow possible. Still, the *jīva* cannot be the locus of *avidyā* because none of the three alternatives about the nature of the *jīva* wherein *avidyā* is said to reside is acceptable: (1) Does *avidyā* reside in the *jīva* as *Brahman* (its natural state)? (2) Does it reside in the *jīva* existing in its psycho-physical organism (the physical body)? (3) Does it reside in the *jīva* comprising its essential nature as qualified by the superimposed aspect?[8]

The Advaitin has said that the *jīva* is a complex entity of which

8. *Śatadūṣaṇī*, topic 40.

knowledge is its true nature and superimposed upon this essential nature is the physical adjunct. Granting this, Vedānta Deśika is contending that none of the above three possibilities is tenable. If one accepts the first alternative, one ends up with *avidyā* being located in *Brahman* and not in the *jīva*. To accept the second alternative leads to the unacceptable conclusion that something inert (*jaḍa*), the physical adjunct, is the locus of *avidyā*. As well, this would mean that *avidyā* would never be removed since the inert never has a conscious desire or the power to remove it. Finally, the last alternative leads to the fallacy of reciprocal dependence. Whether one chooses *avidyā* resting in the *jīva* as qualified by an imagined form (which has been caused by itself), or one chooses *avidyā* residing in the *jīva* as qualified by a form that has been caused by another *avidyā*, the end result is a vicious circle.

A final objection that Vedānta Deśika poses is in regard to *avidyā* itself. He asks: Is *avidyā* one or many? If it is one, as the Vivaraṇa school claims, then with its removal in one *jīva*, it follows that all *jīvas* would be released and universal liberation would occur. If even one *jīva* is not liberated, then *avidyā*, too, must be said to exist and as such there would be no liberation for even one individual.

On the other hand, if *avidyā* is many, as the Bhāmatī school holds, the question becomes: 'Which came first, the *jīva* or *avidyā*?' Either way, this leads to the fallacy of reciprocal dependence. When the *avidyās*, as located in many *jīvas*, are known to be many, it follows that the *jīvas* are many; when the *jīvas* are established to be many, there is a plurality of *avidyās* abiding in them.[9]

Reply 2

Earlier we noted that since both the *jīva* and *avidyā* are beginningless, according to Advaita, it is irrelevant to raise the question of chronological priority of one over the other. Since the two are co-concepts which possess logical tenability only in the context of each other, there is no question as to the logical priority between the *jīva* and *avidyā*. *Avidyā* is, by its very nature, inscrutable.

9. Ibid.

Madhusūdana Sarasvatī replied to Vedānta Deśika's objections regarding the fallacy of reciprocal dependence as applied to the locus of *avidyā*.[10] He asks, 'If the critic says that reciprocal dependence pertains between the *jīva* and *avidyā*, is it in respect of their origin (*utpatti*), knowledge (*jñapti*), or existence (*sthiti*)?'

Mutual dependence cannot obtain between them in respect of their origin because both of them are beginningless. Neither can it pertain to them in respect to their knowledge. *Avidyā* is revealed by knowledge (which is the essential nature of the *jīva*), but the *jīva* (in its true nature) does not require the aid of *avidyā* for knowledge to be revealed—for it is self-luminous. Nor can mutual dependence be said to pertain to them in respect of their existence. *Avidyā* is dependent upon knowledge which is the essential nature of the *jīva* for its existence, but the *jīva* is not dependent upon *avidyā* for its existence. As well, *avidyā* cannot be conceived of apart from the existence of pure Consciousness, while the *jīva* (as it really is) can be conceived of apart from *avidyā*. Therefore, it is fallacious to claim that there is a defect of reciprocal dependence in regard to the *jivā* being the locus of *avidyā*.

It should be observed that most of the critic's objections stem from an incorrect understanding of the Advaitin's doctrine. The *jīva*, as it is in its true nature (*Brahman*, pure Consciousness), is non-different from *Brahman*. This is from the absolute (*pāramārthika*) perspective. But from the relative (*vyāvahārika*) viewpoint, the *jīva* is a complex entity comprised of *Brahman*-knowledge plus *avidyā*. Intrinsically the *jīva* is *Brahman*, though it is different from *Brahman* when viewed through *avidyā*.

OBJECTION 4

Sudarśana offers three major objections to the theory that the *jīva* is the locus of *avidyā*.[11] These are:

(1) It involves the fallacy of infinite regress (*anavasthā*);

(2) Any attempt to overcome the fallacy of infinite regress will involve an acceptance of a basic defect;

(3) Advaita's theory of inexplicability is untenable.

10. *Advaita-siddhi*, p. 585.
11. Vide *Śrutaprakāśikā*, p. 169.

The Fallacy of Infinite Regress

The first objection claims that if the appearance of the world in *Brahman* is illusorily caused by *avidyā*, then *avidyā*, too, must be caused by something different from itself. If one claims that *avidyā* is real, then the non-duality of *Brahman* suffers. Thus, there must be a causal chain which involves the world, *avidyā*, and seemingly a cause for *avidyā*, and so on. To invoke your 'seed-sprout' example does not overcome this objection.

Some Vivaraṇa Advaitins, in order to overcome what they see as a defect in the *jīva*-is-the-locus theory, that is, the defect that since *śruti* texts speak of the *jīva* as eternal and if the *jīva* is not, the gain of unperformed actions and the loss of performed actions may arise, contend that *avidyā* is beginningless. But even this position is untenable in Sudarśana's eyes.

Whether one calls *avidyā* beginningless or not, Sudarśana contends that it requires a basic defect as its cause. And whether one calls the *jīva* beginningless or not, if it comes into existence because of *avidyā*, it is not eternal.

Theory of Inexplicability

Sudarśana continues, it will not help solve these objections to invoke your theory of inexplicability. "Inexplicability means absence of intelligibility in the light of reasoning."[12] Yet, *avidyā* seems to admit of intelligibility because when *Brahman*-knowledge arises, *avidyā* disappears due to a conflict between the two. *Avidyā* could be said to be inexplicable only if it persisted even after the rise of *Brahman*-knowledge. In fact, many intelligible things can be said about *avidyā*. One can say: It doesn't persist after the rise of *Brahman*-knowledge; it does not inhere in a liberated individual; by its very nature it is impure; it is opposed to pure Consciousness.

Advaita claims that *Brahman* is one and non-dual, attributeless and undifferentiated Consciousness, and that *avidyā* is the cause of the appearance of the universe of multiplicity. *Avidyā* is illusory, not real. Its cause too, must be illusory or else, in either example,

12. Ibid., *durghaṭatvaṃ ca anupapannaṃ. durghaṭatvaṃ nāma upapatti-nirapekṣatvam.*

duality would arise. The same must hold true for the cause of the cause of *avidyā* and so on. Thus arises the fallacy of infinite regress.

Sudarśana tries to force the Advaitin into saying that *avidyā* arises due to the *jīva* and the *jīva* arises because of *avidyā*. This would have the effect of going counter to *śruti* texts which call the *jīva* eternal. If the *jīva* comes into existence because of *avidyā*, it is not eternal. As well, if the *jīva* is not eternal, it will mean that the fruits of good and bad actions which were not deserved will accrue to the *jīva* as well as the fruits of good and bad actions which are deserved will not accrue.

A final difficulty involves the fact that if the *jīva* is not eternal, it will not persist until it gains liberation.

Reply 3

No Reciprocal Dependence

The Viśiṣṭādvaitin claims that action (*karma*) and the physical body are mutually related in the same manner in which cause and effect or the seed and its sprout are related in a beginningless series. Without *karma,* there will be no body. Without the body, *karma* is not possible. No one can say which of the two entities came first.

The Advaitin asks the Viśiṣṭādvaitin, 'How is it that you postulate that the defect of reciprocal dependence between *karma* and the body is overcome by an admittance of a beginningless series and, at the same time, say that there is a defect of reciprocal dependence between the *jīva* and *avidyā*?' In short, what applies to your theory should as well apply to your opponent's.

Even if this be your position, the Advaitin contends that the critic's objections are still invalid. The *jīva* is a complex entity as we stated earlier. When the *śruti* texts say that the *jīva* is eternal, they are referring to the essential nature of the *jiva*. That other aspect of the *jīva*, which is caused by *avidyā*, is impermanent. The true nature of the *jīva* should not be confused with its adventitious aspect. Sudarśana's first objection has made this mistake.

The objection that the *jīva*, if not eternal, would lose performed *karmas* and gain unperformed ones is also untenable. So long as the individual is involved in the empirical world, its status is permanent. From this perspective, the karmic laws are inviolate. It is only from the absolute perspective that the *jīva*, in association with *avidyā*, is not eternal. However, from the absolute point of view the *jīva* is not in any way affected by either meritorious or harmful *karmas*. Nothing affects the *jīva* as it really is, in its true state as pure Consciousness.

The Viśiṣṭādvaitin maintains that a certain type of relation exists between *karma* and physical bodies. This type of relation is not the same as that which exists between the *jīva* and *avidyā*. There is a plurality of *karmas* and a plurality of physical bodies. As well, there is a plurality of seeds and sprouts. But, according to the general Vivaraṇa view, there is neither a plurality of *jīvas* nor a plurality of *avidyā*.[13]

No Infinite Regress

It is accepted that because of *avidyā* there is the *jīva*, and because of the *jīva* there is *avidyā*. Both of them are said to be beginningless. However, because both of them are single, there is no causal series possible. Thus, the beginningless series which is alluded to is only figuratively used.[14]

All of these entities (*jīva*, *avidyā*, *karma*, physical bodies, seeds, sprouts) are similar in the respect that the question over which one came first cannot be answered. It is in this respect that they are said to be beginningless. According to Advaita, that which has no birth, has no death or end. Thus, it can't mean absence of birth in this respect, for both the *jīva* and *avidyā* can be terminated. Beginningless means, in such a context, not absence of birth, but in the sense that their beginning cannot be ascertained.

No Basic Defect

Sudarśana thinks that *avidyā* requires a cause for its own appearance. Even as *avidyā* is illusory, the cause of *avidyā* must also be illusory so as not to vitiate the non-duality of *Brāhman*.

Śruti says that *avidyā* comes to be associated with *Brahman* of its own accord. "*Māyā*, i.e. *avidyā*, comes into existence by itself."[15]

13. Vide *Vivaraṇa-prameya-saṅgraha*, p. 243.
14. *Śrī-śaṅkarāśaṅkara-bhāṣya-vimarśaḥ*, p. 282.
15. *Nṛsiṃhapūrvatāpanīya Upaniṣad*, IX.3.

Thus, while *avidyā* is the cause of the universe of multiplicity, *avidyā*, itself, has no cause. Inscrutable as it is, it accounts for itself as well as for the illusory world of plurality. Thus, there is no need to posit a basic defect as the cause of *avidyā.*

INEXPLICABILITY

Sudarśana's understanding of what the Advaitin means by inexplicability is incorrect. The Advaitin does not say that *avidyā* is inexplicable due to its sublatability by knowledge, its being the cause of the world and its being illusory. It is inexplicable because of its association with *Brahman. Avidyā* is everything; *Brahman* is not. It is false, insentient, sublatable. *Brahman* is real, sentient, unsublatable. The mystery concerns their seeming relationship.

Avidyā is inexplicable from an empirical perspective. Thus, it is no argument to contend that it should persist even in the state of liberation. In that state, *avidyā* is totally non-existent.

Avidyā, the inexplicable, gives rise to the inexplicable world. The gross world cannot come into existence by itself. It needs a cause. Its cause is *avidyā*, which is subtle. From the unmanifest (*avidyā*) comes the manifest (world). Thus, even if the world needed a cause to come into existence, *avidyā* would not. The gross always proceeds from the subtle and not the other way around.

ĀŚRAYA-ANUPAPATTI 2

The Vivaraṇa school holds that *Brahman* is the locus of *avidyā*, even as darkness is in the house which it conceals. It appears that the first polemical discussions on the subject were introduced by Sureśvara with special reference to the views of Maṇḍana.[16] The *Naiṣkarmya-siddhi* states:

> Hence we conclude, as the only remaining alternative, that it is the Self alone which is both the locus (*āśraya*) of and the object (*viṣaya*) concealed by ignorance.[17]

What kept the dialectics alive was Vācaspati's *Bhāmatī*, which tried to reconcile Śaṅkara's views with those of Maṇḍana. So the

16. *Naiṣkarmya-siddhi.*
17. Ibid., 3.1.

debate continued, from teacher to pupil, within the Advaita lineage until the Viśiṣṭādvaitins took up the polemics too.

Objection 1

Rāmānuja dismissed the Bhāmatī view of *jīva-ajñāna-vāda* in one sentence. But he went into great length and subtlety to refute the *brahma-ajñāna-vāda*. His first objection states:

> Neither can it be *Brahman*, for It is self-proved and of the nature of knowledge and so opposed to ignorance. Since Nescience is destroyed by Knowledge, the two cannot co-exist.[18]

This means that *Brahman* cannot be the locus of *avidyā* because *Brahman*, Which is of the nature of self-luminous knowledge, is opposed to *avidyā*, which is ignorance. Just as light is opposed to darkness, so must knowledge be opposed to ignorance. You, yourself, admit that ignorance is sublated by knowledge. Therefore, *Brahman* cannot be the locus of *avidyā*.

Reply 1

According to the Advaitin, this objection is untenable. The Advaitin's true position has been misrepresented. A correct understanding of the doctrine would know that the Advaitin makes a distinction between *Brahman*-knowledge or the Self (*svarūpa-jñāna*) and mental cognitions (*vṛtti-jñāna*).

Avidyā is the potency of *Brahman*. It is the cause of both valid and erroneous cognitions, which are but modes (*vṛttis*) of the mind. The mind, being insentient, produces only insentient modifications. These modifications appear to be sentient due to the reflection of consciousness therein. What is important to note is that the mind is said to possess the power of revealing things which are presented to it only by virtue of the borrowed light of *Brahman*-knowledge reflected therein. Thus, mind, mental modes, and *avidyā* are all revealed by *Brahman*-knowledge. But *Brahman*-knowledge is self-illumined and not revealed by anything else. Only if it, too, were revealed by something else would the fallacy of infinite regress pertain.

The upshot of the whole position is that it is only *vṛtti-jñāna*

18. *Śrī-bhāṣya* I.1.1, p. 55.

(mental cognition) which is opposed to *avidyā*, and not *svarūpa-jñāna*. *Brahman* is of the nature of knowledge and reveals everything, including *avidyā*. There is no conflict between the revealer—*Brahman*-knowledge (*svarūpa-jñāna*) and the revealed—*avidyā* (*vṛtti-jñāna*).

OBJECTION 2

Rāmānuja continues the objection saying that even though you divide knowledge into two types (*svarūpa-jñāna* and *vṛtti-jñāna*), after all, knowledge is knowledge. Even though the qualifiers differ, since knowledge is all one body, how can you claim that one type of knowledge is opposed to *avidyā*, while another is not?

Rāmānuja says,

> It cannot be said that what is opposed to Nescience is not the knowledge which is *Brahman's* nature but the knowledge that *Brahman* is pure Knowledge, for there is no difference between the two, viz. the knowledge which is *Brahman's* nature and the knowledge about *Brahman's* true nature, both being self-luminous and so the latter cannot be said to be particularly opposed to Nescience and the other not.[19]

REPLY 2

Advaita acknowledges that knowledge of an object generally removes the ignorance of that object. Thus, knowledge and ignorance are opposed to one another. However, knowledge can remove ignorance only if it relates to the same content (*viṣaya*) referred to by ignorance. The knowledge obtained is called *svarūpa-viṣaya-jñāna*. This type of knowledge comes through a mental mode. It is the same knowledge as what we earlier called *vṛtti-jñāna* or modal knowledge.

Modal knowledge of a rock or any other empirical entity takes the form of a fragmented mode. However, knowledge of *Brahman* requires a special type of mode (*vṛtti*) because *Brahman* is not fragmented. This impartite knowledge is called *akhaṇḍākāra-vṛtti-jñāna*.

It is *vṛtti-jñāna* (also known as *svarūpa-viṣaya-jñāna*) which re-

19. Ibid., pp. 55-56.

moves *avidyā*, and not *svarūpa-jñāna* (which is the essential nature of *Brahman*). Thus, Rāmānuja is incorrect to say that there is no difference between the two types of knowledge recognized by the Advaitins.

It is strange that Rāmānuja raises this objection, for he himself maintains that there are two types of knowledge. He acknowledges both knowledge which is constitutive of the self (*dharmi-jñāna*) and knowledge which is attributive of the self (*dharma-bhūta-jñāna*). What is good for the goose should also be good for the gander. This distinction will be explored in greater depth later.

The critic may ask why *Brahman*-knowledge (as it is) cannot remove *avidyā* and yet *Brahman*-knowledge (as being reflected through a mental mode) can. The Advaitin puts forth an analogy about the sun and its power. The light of the sun, when passed through a magnifying glass, can burn a combustible substance while that same light, by itself, cannot. There is a speciality about knowledge reflected in a mental mode—even as there is a speciality about certain types of dreams. Nightmares possess the power to awaken the dreamer while other types of dreams do not.

A final note about modal knowledge is that, while it is admitted to be valid (*pramā*), it is not real (*paramārtha*). If it were real, non-duality would be compromised. It is said to be not real because it also disappears when *avidyā*, which is its material cause, is destroyed.

Objection 3

Rāmānuja's third objection about positing that *Brahman* is the locus of *avidyā* concerns the very possibility of knowledge of *Brahman* obtained through a mental mode. He says:

> Moreover, knowledge about *Brahman's* true nature is not possible, for that would make *Brahman* an object of knowledge and the Advaitins deny it.[20]

If *Brahman* is known through modal knowledge, then *Brahman* is an object of knowledge. Per Advaita, *Brahman* Which is of the nature of knowledge, cannot be the object of another knowledge. The knower can never become the known and still remain the

20. Ibid., p. 56.

knower. If this is the case, then it follows, according to Rāmānuja, that 'there cannot be a knowledge which has *Brahman* as its object.[21] If *Brahman* is an object of knowledge, then *Brahman* is inert (*jaḍa*) because you Advaitins say that whatever is an object of knowledge is material or insentient.

Or, if you say that *Brahman* is not knowable, then you should give up your distinction between two types of knowledge. The consequence of this means that *akhaṇḍākāra-vṛtti-jñāna*, impartite knowledge of *Brahman*, is impossible in contra-distinction to what the Advaitin claims.

Reply 3

This type of criticism involves a misunderstanding of the Advaitin's doctrine. First, it must be understood that *Brahman* is never an object of knowledge in the sense in which a rock is. Second, as long as an individual is enmeshed in the empirical world of multiplicity (which is based upon *avidyā*), *Brahman* (which is of the nature of knowledge) remains concealed by *avidyā*. When this is the case, it is appropriate to speak of *Brahman* as being apprehended by *akhaṇḍākāra-vṛtti-jñāna*.

According to Advaita, two conditions are necessary for something to be said to be an object of knowledge. Both the mental mode (*vṛtti*) and the knowledge (*phala*) reflected therein are needed for cognizing an object. However, to have knowledge of *Brahman*, all that is necessary is the special mode or *akhaṇḍākāra-vṛtti-jñāna*. This is so because *Brahman* itself is knowledge and thus the *phala* is not needed. It is in this sense that the Advaitin says that *Brahman* is not an object of knowledge. Thus, even though *Brahman* is not known in the manner in which a rock is known, still, *Brahman* is apprehended through a (unique) mental mode.[22] Though, from the final or established position of Advaita, truly speaking *Brahman* does not need to be known at all—since *Brahman* is all there is, an already established fact. The above manner of reply is but a concession to a philosophical dialogue from an empirical perspective.

21. Vide *Śrī-bhāṣya*, I.1.1., p. 56.
22. Vide *Śrī-śaṅkarāśaṅkara-bhāṣya-vimarśaḥ*, p. 279. *nitya-jñānasya brahmaṇaḥ anitya-vṛttijñāna-sadbhāvāt*.

OBJECTION 4

Rāmānuja's final objection to the view that *Brahman* is the locus of *avidyā* is a lengthy one and raises a number of objections. His contention is that Advaita cannot explain how ignorance of *Brahman's* true nature is ever removed.

How does the individual, sunk in *avidyā*, gain knowledge of *Brahman*? Supposedly, according to Advaita, *Brahman*-knowledge is not opposed to *avidyā*. Thus, it will not remove ignorance of *Brahman*. As well, Rāmānuja has argued that *vṛtti-jñāna* will not remove this ignorance because *Brahman* cannot be an object of knowledge. The Advaitin has replied to these two objections.

So Rāmānuja offers another objection. He says,

> If it be said that what destroys Nescience is the knowledge of the unreality of manifoldness, then such knowledge cannot destroy the ignorance of *Brahman*, for this knowledge and Nescience do not refer to the same object.[23]

If one knows that the world is false, will that knowledge remove one's ignorance of *Brahman*? The maxim is, knowledge removes ignorance. However, in this case, they relate to two different contents. Knowledge here relates to 'what is other than *Brahman*'. Ignorance, in this case, relates to 'the true nature of *Brahman*'. Thus, the former knowledge cannot dispel the latter ignorance.

Rāmānuja continues the objection:

> It may, however, be argued that ignorance about *Brahman's* nature is nothing but regarding that there are other real things besides *Brahman* and therefore this ignorance is destroyed when other objects are shown to be unreal.[24]

The knowledge that the world (which is other than *Brahman*) is false will no doubt remove the ignorance as a result of which one thinks that the world is real. This is obvious. But, this knowledge cannot remove the ignorance about the true nature of *Brahman*, for its content is different from the content of *Brahman*. *Brahman* is self-proved and no contrary notion about It exists.

23. Ibid.
24. Ibid.

REPLY 4

The Advaitin maintains that one must have knowledge of the world in order to say that it is other than *Brahman.* If one does not know that the world exists, one cannot label it true or false. The Advaitin also maintains that one must know the real nature of *Brahman* in order to say that the world, which is other than *Brahman,* is false. As well, it is incumbent that ignorance be removed before one knows the real nature of *Brahman.* This must be achieved through an *akhaṇḍākāra-vṛtti.* Consequently, *ipso facto*, when an individual knows that the world, which is other than *Brahman*, is false, one cannot be ignorant of the true nature of *Brahman.*

Thus, the Vivaraṇa position that *Brahman*-knowledge is not opposed to *avidyā* is tenable and *Brahman* can well be the locus for ignorance.

One final note here. The Advaitin asks, 'How do we know there is *avidyā*?' It is not known through any valid means of knowledge (*pramāṇa*), because anything which is known through a valid means of knowledge must be valid and real. What is real cannot be sublated and therefore liberation would be rendered impossible.

An important epistemological point is involved here. It concerns the Advaitin's distinction between knowledge produced by the internal organ (*antaḥkaraṇa-vṛtti*) and knowledge produced by the witness self (*avidyā-vṛtti*). In perception by the internal organ, the mind takes the form of the object; the object and the mind become identified. But the mind has no role in *avidyā-vṛtti.* The object exists, knowledge exists, but the knowing is done by the witness self (*sākṣin*). There is no sense-object contact here.

The Advaitin says that *avidyā* is revealed by the witness self (*sākṣin*). To object that if it is revealed by the *sākṣin,* it cannot hide or destroy that on which it is dependent, is fallacious. Three things are known to be revealed by the witness self alone (*kevala-sākṣi-bhāṣya*): illusory objects (*prātibhāsika*) such as mirages or rope-snakes; subjective internal states of the mind, e.g., pain or pleasure; and ignorance (*avidyā*).

Thus, there are a couple of points to be noted here. *Avidyā* is not a product of the mind. Illusions are not a product of the mind. Both are revealed by the witness self. The mind cannot know itself; it is the *sākṣin* who knows it. The *sākṣin* or *Brahman*-knowledge reveals both valid and invalid cognitions alike. It is antagonistic to none.

Objection 5

Vedānta Deśika examined the Advaita theory that *Brahman* is the locus of *avidyā* and raised a number of objections. These can be grouped under: (1) *Brahman* is not the knower; (2) *Brahman* is self-luminous; (3) *Brahman* is eternally free; (4) *Brahman* is omniscient.[25]

(1) Ignorance must reside in the knower, or that which is the substrate of knowledge, if it is to be removed by the said knowledge. We observed this maxim in an earlier objection. Knowledge of 'x' cannot remove the ignorance located in 'y'. The Advaitin claims that *Brahman* is not the knower and hence it cannot be the locus of *avidyā*.

It is true that *Brahman* is the knower in an illusory sense, but this will not alleviate the problem. For, in the state of deep sleep, the illusory "I" is extinguished and *Brahman*/*Ātman* will have to be acknowledged as the locus of *avidyā*.

(2) The Advaitin says that *Brahman* is self-luminous. It is of the nature of knowledge and opposed to *avidyā* like light is to darkness. How then can it be the locus of *avidyā*? And if it does allow the presence of ignorance in it, how can this ignorance then be removed?

(3) The Advaitin claims that *Brahman* is eternally free. If this is the case, then how can *Brahman* be the locus of *avidyā*? Bondage is but another name for 'being associated with ignorance'. Liberation is defined as the 'end of ignorance'. Isn't it self-contradictory to claim that the eternally free *Brahman* is the seat of bondage (*avidyā*)?

(4) *Brahman* is said to be omniscient. Whatever is omniscient cannot have ignorance or its omniscience is compromised. Either one knows everything or, if there is something one does not know, one is not omniscient.

Reply 5

These four objections are based upon a misunderstanding of the

25. *Śatadūṣaṇī, Vāda* 19.

Advaitin's position. The first three criticisms fail to acknowledge the distinction between *Brahman* as It is and *Brahman* associated with *avidyā*, as well as the distinction between *svarūpa-jñāna* and *vṛtti-jñāna*. The fourth objection was answered by Sureśvara saying that in view of the falsity of *avidyā*, *Brahman's* omniscience has not been compromised.[26]

In actuality, it is not the *nirguṇa Brahman* That is omniscient, but *Īśvara* or the *saguṇa Brahman*. The correct position is that nescience is located in pure Consciousness, but manifests itself in the *jīva* associated with its limiting adjuncts. The property of being the locus is only assumptive. There is oneness between the original and the reflection, though defects are superimposed upon the reflection. We noted earlier that defects which appear on the face of an individual through defects in the mirror, do not affect the individual. Likewise, though *avidyā* is located in *Brahman*, it in no way hinders Its omniscience.

Objection 6

The Bhāmatī school asks, 'Is *avidyā* located in the whole of *Brahman* or only in a part?' It cannot cover the whole of *Brahman* for, upon the realization of *Brahman*, there is no *avidyā*. If *avidyā* occupies only a part of *Brahman*, then the question becomes: Does the part of *Brahman* that *avidyā* occupies belong to *Brahman* as Its part? Is that part real? Or is it an unreal superimposition?

If that part is real, the *śruti* declaration that *Brahman* is partless would be invalidated. If that part is an unreal superimposition, then the question becomes: Is that part of the nature of the *jīva* and *Īśvara* or is it of the nature of the universe of multiplicity?

This part of *Brahman* cannot be identified with the universe of multiplicity. Neither can it be of the nature of the *jīva* or *Īśvara* as they are conditioned by *avidyā*. It is not a mere void. It cannot be of the nature of *avidyā* for that would entail an infinite regress. There is no other alternative except to conclude that, from an empirical view, *avidyā* must reside in a part of *Brahman*.

There are *śruti* passages which support such a conclusion:

> The *Veda* declares that all beings, sentient
> and non-sentient, constitute but a quarter of

26. *Bṛhadāraṇyaka-upaniṣad-bhāṣya-vārttika* II.1220.

> *Brahman*, three-quarters remaining unobscured, and self-effulgent.[27]

The *Brahma-sūtra* says:

> *Brahman* transcends the cosmos which is but a product, a modification.[28]

Though *Brahman* is partless, attributeless, one, and non-dual, It appears as if divided and possessed of parts. This is due to the inscrutable *avidyā*.

REPLY 6

These objections are based on a misconception. *Brahman* alone can be the locus of *avidyā*. All that is not *Brahman* is of the nature of ignorance and it does not make any sense to say that ignorance is located in what is of the nature of ignorance. Ignorance has no scope for its work of concealment in respect of the world of multiplicity. Secondly, both knowledge and ignorance must have the same locus. We observed this earlier. Thirdly, what owes its very existence to *avidyā*, cannot be its support. Finally, a locus must have a nature of its own, independent of what is located in it.

One final word on the locus of *avidyā*. It seems that the question of where *avidyā* resides is rather simple from the Advaitin's perspective. *Avidyā* is essentially unreal and thus it cannot, and need not, have a real residence. This point cannot be stressed enough. It is only from the ignorant individual's perspective that the question arises at all. Clearly, from that perspective, *avidyā* appears to reside in the *jīva* who is perceiving the world of multiplicity. But, is not the *jīva* non-different from *Brahman*? Isn't that the bottom line of Advaita? Thus, it is equally true to hold that the *jīva* or *Brahman*, when correctly understood, is the locus of *avidyā*.

27. *Ṛg Veda* X.90.4.
28. *Brahma-sūtra* IV.4.19.

CHAPTER THREE

THE UNTENABILITY OF OBSCURATION

A CRITIQUE OF RĀMĀNUJA'S TIRODHĀNA-ANUPAPATTI AGAINST THE ADVAITA CONCEPTION OF AVIDYĀ

INTRODUCTION

According to Advaita, *Brahman/Ātman* is pure, non-dual, non-relational, non-differentiated, self-luminous Consciousness. Due to the obscuring and projecting powers of *avidyā*, it appears in the two forms of *Īśvara* and *jīva*. The question becomes, even if *Brahman* (or the *jīva* in its essential nature) is the locus of *avidyā*: How can it be the content of ignorance? How can that which is constantly, self-luminously manifesting itself be the content of *avidyā*? In regard to a rock which is manifesting itself to an individual, no one would say that it is not. So how can that which is ever manifest be said to be covered by ignorance? Rāmānuja says:

> It is not possible to ascribe the experience
> of ignorance to *Brahman* Which is by nature one,
> eternal, free, self-luminous consciousness, for
> It is of the nature of self-luminous
> consciousness.[1]

If *Brahman* is declared to be self-luminous consciousness and yet is obscured by ignorance, the question is: What does it mean to say that *Brahman* is obscured? Does it mean that the self-luminous is no longer luminous? If this obscuration is due to an outside agent, then it follows that when the consciousness which is *Brahman's* very nature is obscured, *Brahman* Itself is destroyed.

Brahman is consciousness. One is neither an object nor a subject. Thus, to say that *Brahman* is consciousness means that *Brahman*-as-consciousness is not conscious of anything—whether pertaining to knowledge or ignorance. *Brahman* is not an experi-

1. *Śrī-bhāṣya* I.1.1, p. 64.

ence of something but experience qua experience. Therefore, it is wrong to say that *Brahman* is conscious of *avidyā*.

The Jīva

According to Advaita, it is the *jīva* who is the knower, the subject of knowledge and ignorance. Even though Advaita claims that the *jīva* is non-different from *Brahman*, it does not say so in regard to the *jīva* in its empirical condition. It is only the *jīva* in its essential nature that is non-different from *Brahman*. Thus, what holds true for the *jīva* in the empirical condition, does not hold true for *Brahman*.

Īśvara 1

If *Brahman* does not have the experience of *avidyā*, is it possible to say that *Īśvara* does? Though *Īśvara* is a knower, He cannot be said to experience ignorance in the way as the *jīva* does. *Īśvara* is omniscient while the *jīva* has limited knowledge. Because *Īśvara* knows everything, He can't say 'I am ignorant' in the same manner as an individual can.

When *Īśvara* is said to have the experience of ignorance, it means something other than what it means to say that the individual has the experience of ignorance. The *jīva's* experience means, 'I am ignorant' about some experience or cognition. But *Īśvara's* experience is different. He has no experience or cognition to the effect, 'I am ignorant'. Yet, *Īśvara* is omniscient and His experience takes the form of, 'this is ignorance'. He is the witness to ignorance, as well as to every other experience and cognition, valid or invalid. Thus the *śruti* says, "The other looks on without eating."[2]

Because *Īśvara* associated with the adjunct of *avidyā*, He is the knower. As such, He has the cognition of everything. While the individual knows through the internal organ, *Īśvara* knows through the modes of *avidyā* (*avidyā-vṛtti*).

Thus, we can conclude that while the *jīva* has an experience of *avidyā* as 'I am ignorant', and *Īśvara* has an experience of *avidyā* as 'this is ignorance', *Brahman* does not have the experience of *avidyā* in any form whatsoever.

2. *Muṇḍaka Upaniṣad* III.i.1.

ĪŚVARA 2

A critic may argue in a different manner to show that Advaita's position regarding *Īśvara's* experience of *avidyā* is untenable. It is generally held that a valid cognition generated by a *pramāṇa* is opposed in nature to ignorance. The question raised is: Does *Īśvara* have valid cognitions? The consequences of this become: If He does, then He cannot have the experience of ignorance and if He doesn't, then He cannot be omniscient.

There is one more point to be noted in this argument. *Śruti* is accepted as a *pramāṇa* on the ground that it gives rise to valid cognitions (which remove ignorance). To say that valid cognitions do not remove ignorance would be to jeopardize not only *śruti*, but also liberation. If *avidyā* cannot be removed, then liberation is impossible and there is no need of Scripture.

Advaita accepts that cognitions generated by a valid means of knowledge do destroy *avidyā*. But, they can do so fully only in the absence of any obstacle. As well, valid cognitions are of two kinds: mediate (*parokṣa*) and immediate (*aparokṣa*). *Avidyā*, too, can be spoken of as of two kinds: *avidyā*-which-conceals and *avidyā*-which-projects. These derive from the two powers of *avidyā*, *āvaraṇa* and *vikṣepa*.

There is a corresponding terminology to the two powers of *avidyā*. Sometimes they are spoken of as: *nirmāṇa-śakti* or the power to produce and project, and *moha-śakti* or the power to delude. The former is said to be the power *Īśvara* uses to construct the universe. The latter is what induces individuals to accept duality as the Truth.

Avidyā-which-conceals functions in two ways. It may conceal the existence of an object or it may conceal the direct cognition of an object. In the former sense one may say, '*Brahman* does not exist'. In the latter sense one may say, 'I do not see *Brahman*'. The distinction is very important. Mediate cognitions remove the former type of concealment, while immediate cognitions remove the latter type, e.g., a person may believe that *Brahman* does not exist because the existence aspect of *Brahman* is concealed from him. By taking advantage of literature, other's arguments and reflection, he may become convinced that *Brahman* exists.

By believing that *Brahman* exists, this knowledge is indirect or mediate. This mediate knowledge has removed that aspect of ignorance which was concealing the existence of *Brahman*. When immediate cognition (through *śruti*) of *Brahman* occurs, that aspect of ignorance that concealed a direct cognition of *Brahman* is removed.

Now, the question is: What is it that removes *avidyā*-which-projects? According to Advaitins, it is that same immediate cognition of *Brahman*—only there must not be any obstacle to it in the form of accumulated effects of past deeds (*prārabdha-karma*). The Advaitin's conception of a liberated-in-life individual *jīvan-mukta*) illustrates this point.

A *jīvanmukta* who has realized his identity with *Brahman* still remains in the world, though not of it. Such an individual knows the truth because he has uncovered the two veils of *avidyā*. But since he continues to dwell in a physical body (which continues due to past *karma*), he observes the empirical world while knowing full well that it is illusory and exists because of the projecting power of *avidyā*. He remains a witness to the world until *prārabdha-karma* has run out and then he drops his physical form.

Like the *jīva*, we may speak of the *prārabdha-karma* of *Īśvara*, strange as this may sound. Certainly the Lord is not bound to His actions in the sense in which the *jīva* is. However, since *Īśvara* creates, maintains, and rules the world, He is undoubtedly an agent. And if He is an agent, He must also be an enjoyer of the consequences of His actions.

Unlike the *jīva*, *Īśvara* is not bound by His deeds. As the *śruti* says, "He is the wielder of *māyā*."[3] The obstacle that prevents the removal of the projecting power of *avidyā* for *Īśvara* is the persistence of *karmas* which have given rise to the physical bodies of all the *jīvas*. This is due to the fact that *Īśvara*, as Lord of the universe, is connected with it. He must continue to be the witness of the world's appearance until all *jīvas* have attained liberation. Unlike the *jīvanmukta*, who only has to wait for his physical body to fall before attaining final liberation, *Īśvara* must wait until the final termination of the entire gross physical body of the universe.

Another difference between the *jīvanmukta* and *Īśvara* has to do with the fact that *Īśvara* is one who is ever-liberated in life

3. *Śvetāśvatara Upaniṣad* IV.10.

while the *jīvanmukta* has to attain liberation-in-life by attaining *Brahman*-knowledge.

Īśvara and the *jīva* do differ. However, according to the Advaitin, both of them are conditioned entities with a living status. It is true that in their essential nature they are both identical with *Brahman*, as pure, undifferentiated Consciousness. It is also true that they are both, limited as it were, due to their association with *avidyā*. Their difference is, *Īśvara* is omniscient and, though witness to everything, is not fooled by the appearance of anything. He is subject to projection (*vikṣepa*) though there is no concealment (*āvaraṇa*) for Him. The *jīva*, on the other hand, is subject to both concealment and projection.

Brahman

The argument against *Brahman* being the content of *avidyā* revolves around the view that the locus of knowledge must be different from the content of knowledge. Using this principle, it means that the locus of ignorance must be different from the content of ignorance. If this holds true, then *Brahman* could not be held to be both the locus and content of *avidyā*.

We observed earlier, the Advaitin's reply to this objection. Taking their stand upon the undeniable fact of individual experience, the Advaitins point to the two common experiences expressed in the sayings, 'I know myself', and 'I do not know myself'. In both instances the same object ("I") is both the locus and object of knowledge or ignorance. This holds true, from an empirical point of view, whether about *Brahman* or the empirical individual.

On the other hand, concealment is possible only with reference to a luminous entity. Everything else is insentient, already obscured, and thus in no need of an external cause of obscuration. Hence, it may well be concluded that *Brahman* alone has the possibility of being veiled. Thus, *Brahman* alone is the content of *avidyā*.

Avidyā

Why should an individual accept *avidyā* at all? First, because it is a self-evident fact of experience. Everyone has the experience of saying, 'I do not know'. Second, it is everyone's experience that *avidyā* is manifested by, and manifests in return, Consciousness. Always in conjunction with the experience, 'I do not know', is the knowledge, 'I know that I do not know'. This proves that there is no *avidyā*, pure and simple, but that it is always manifested by Consciousness.

If one were to enquire how *avidyā*, though dependent upon *Brahman*, can conceal *Brahman*, the analogy is put forth—'like clouds covering the sun'. Clouds are known to hide the sun from view. However, the clouds never really totally conceal the sun because it is the sun which makes them possible in the first place. Clouds are dependent upon the sun's heat, just as *avidyā* is dependent upon *Brahman*.

If one were to enquire how such a small entity like *avidyā* can conceal such a large entity like *Brahman*, the analogy would be given—'like a finger hiding the sun'. Though very small in comparison to the sun, when a finger is put before one's eye, it is able to conceal the sun from one's vision.

The mysterious power of *avidyā* is called *durghaṭatva*. It is that which makes the impossible possible. Though it has no ultimate reality itself, yet it can seemingly project creation and produce things. Seemingly omnipotent, it vanishes when one enquires into *Brahman*. To pursue it is only to fall deeper and deeper into its morass. *Brahman* must be enquired into for there is no solution to *avidyā*, only dissolution. Contrary to what the critics say, this facet of *avidyā* is not a defect, but an ornament.

Avidyā is spoken of in three ways, according to the Advaita tradition. (1) For the common individual, who lacks the ability to discern the real from the unreal, the world is real. The question does not even arise as to whether the world around them is real or not. To this type of individual, *avidyā* is spoken of as *vāstavī*—that which is real. (2) For the individual who possesses reason and enquires into the reality of the world, *avidyā* becomes inexplicable. This type of individual cannot say whether the world is real or not, and thus continues to enquire into its ontological status. To such a one, *avidyā* is spoken of as *anirvacanīya*—inexplicable. (3) For the realized individuals, the world no longer possesses the capacity to delude. Though the world is perceived, its chains are broken. For such a one, *avidyā* is spoken of as *tuccha*—non-existent, false, unreal.

ADHYĀSA

Avidyā has two powers of obscuring (*āvaraṇa*) and projecting (*vikṣepa*). It obscures or conceals *Brahman*, which is of the nature of knowledge, and projects the world of multiplicity, which is insentient.

In order for *avidyā* to conceal *Brahman* and project the unreal universe of multiplicity thereon, there must be: (1) a residual impression caused by a cognition of an object; (2) a defect in the object of knowledge; (3) a defect in the cognizer; (4) a defect in the instrument of valid knowledge; and (5) a knowledge of the general nature alone of the substrate without a knowledge of its particularities. For example, (1) an individual who has never seen water before will never superimpose it upon the desert; (2) there must be a similarity between the substrate of superimposition (sand) and what is superimposed thereon (water); (3) the subject, being thirsty, has a desire for water; (4) the eyes see waves of heat; (5) the general nature of the sand is observed but its particularity is obscured. The 'this' which is observed is sand, but the particularity of it is observed to be water. If the sand was not observed as 'this', no superimposition as 'water' would take place.

Sometimes Advaitins say that there are four conditions which must be met to observe superimposition: (1) there must be ignorance of the real nature of the object perceived; (2) there must be a predisposition to see the superimposed cognition; (3) there must be a mistaken impression; and (4) conditions must be favourable.

Critics of Advaita attack their doctrine of superimposition along the following lines. What is the residual impression which the individual superimposes? You say that 'I'-ness, bondage, etc. are superimposed upon the Self. But these things are not real and as such, how can they be superimposed?

The Advaitin replies, what is superimposed need not be real. All that is required is an impression of a prior cognition. Even the residual impression of an illusory object may serve as a cause of superimposition. It is not necessary to have seen real water to superimpose it upon the desert. It is enough if one has seen even illusory water produced by a magician.

The three defects given were in the object, the instrument and the seer. If the defect superimposed is 'I'-ness, bondage, etc., the

Self must play the part of all the three (since all else comes under the category of the superimposed). Yet, according to the Advaitin, the Self is pure Consciousness and predication of defects therein is impossible. So how can there be a defect superimposed thereon?

The Advaitin replies, even in the flawless Self, there is the defect of *avidyā*. It may be unreal, but it appears nonetheless. Proof of this is the scriptural passage:

> Just as those who do not know the land, though repeatedly passing over the hidden treasure of gold, do not attain it, even so all these people go to Brahmaloka day after day, but do not attain it, being obstructed by the non-real (nescience).[4]

Earlier we noted that *avidyā* is inscrutable, inexplicable. To the mind, which lives by dividing, distinguishing and discriminating, *avidyā* is a Pandora's Box of contradictions. The Advaitin, instead of languishing over this inability to explain the 'how' of ignorance, revels in the knowledge that this is the example par excellence of the intellect's demand not to be satisfied with mere observations of fact and to attempt to explain them. Whitehead said, "Curiosity is the craving of reason that the facts discriminated in experience be understood. It means the refusal to be satisfied with the bare welter of fact."[5]

However, the mind can never achieve a finality in its adventure through the realm of thought. Today's certainties of science are tomorrow's delusions. The mind is a molder, a manipulator which only dimly discerns and generally misdescribes and wrongly associates through an ever-elusive certainty. The intellect is but another name for 'desire'.

The 'how' which the scientific mind seeks to know is nothing more than a precise definition of the 'that'. Yet, even at this end of thought, any religion which attempts to explain final causes has only shifted the problem from the antecedent to the consequent. Reason is fundamentally limited. Be it Materialism or Idealism, discursive thinking cannot transcend its own limitations.

Knowing full well that the mind (which is a product of *avidyā*) cannot ever grasp that which lies outside the narrow constricting

4. *Chāndogya Upaniṣad* VIII.iii.2.
5. A.N. Whitehead, *Adventures of Ideas*, p. 180.

boundaries of duality, the Advaitin is content to dissolve the problem of *avidyā*, and does not attempt to solve it.

RĀMĀNUJA'S TIRODHĀNA-ANUPAPATTI

OBJECTION

Rāmānuja's second major objection to the Advaitin's doctrine of *avidyā* is concerned with the question of the concealment of the nature of *Brahman*. He asks, 'What is the meaning of concealment?' It must mean either preventing the origination of light/knowledge/Consciousness or the destruction of the existing light/knowledge/Consciousness.

> Again, when the Advaitins say that *Brahman* Which is self-luminous pure Consciousness is covered by Nescience, they only establish that *Brahman* is destroyed; for this covering means either an obstruction to the origination of consciousness or the destruction of what exists.[6]

The Advaitin's claim is that *Brahman*, Whose nature is Consciousness, is concealed by *avidyā*. If this is accepted, then it follows that the individual (the *jīva*, whose essential nature is *Brahman*) is concealed by ignorance and experiences that ignorance. It is this claim that Rāmānuja is objecting to.

The Advaitin says that *Brahman* is knowledge (*jñāna-svarūpa*) and this knowledge is ever self-luminous (*prakāśa-svarūpa*). However, according to Rāmānuja, this puts the Advaitin between the horns of a dilemma. There are two possibilities open to them. They may say that concealment of Consciousness means obstructing the origination of consciousness or it means destroying the Consciousness that exists.

Obviously the first alternative is unacceptable. There is no possibility of saying that *avidyā* prevents the origination of knowledge because this goes against your own definition of knowledge as being eternal and non-originated. If anything has an origination, according to you, then it also has an end. *Brahman*, therefore, cannot have an origination. And if *Brahman* does not have an

6. *Śrī-bhāṣya* I.1.1, p. 57.

origination, then how can you say that *avidyā* can prevent or obscure what is eternally present and self-manifest?[7]

The second alternative is a favourite of Rāmānuja. Clearly he is attempting to lay the foundation for the Viśiṣṭādvaitin doctrine here. He continues, the concealment of Consciousness (*svarūpa-tirodhāna*) thus must mean the absence of Consciousness (*svarūpa-aprakāśa*)—which, *ipso facto*, means *svarūpa-nāśa*—the destruction of the existing light/knowledge/Consciousness.

We know that light and darkness are antagonistic to each other. We know that knowledge and ignorance oppose each other. When the Advaitin's eternally self-luminous Consciousness ceases to be luminous due to concealment, obviously this means that *Brahman's* eternal nature has been lost! And what applies to *Brahman's* nature, must also apply to *Brahman.* The Advaitin could at least have saved *Brahman* if he had been prepared to admit that knowledge/Consciousness is only an attribute of *Brahman,* for the loss of an attribute does not mean the loss of whatever it is an attribute of. But, the loss of the essential nature of a thing, means the loss of the thing itself.

Reply

Rāmānuja has ingeniously paved the way for a *Brahman* with attributes. By twisting the meaning of the word 'concealment', he has seemingly placed the Advaitin in a quandary. However, a little commonsense reflection will be in order.

Even in ordinary life, to say that there is concealment/obscuration requires the help of light/knowledge/Consciousness. For example, to observe that the sun is obscured or concealed from one's vision by clouds is not to say that the sun has been destroyed. Concealment does not mean destruction in the ordinary meaning of the term. So by what authority does Rāmānuja ignore the ordinary day-to-day meaning of the word and give it a meaning all his own?

The same may be said of *Brahman.* When *Brahman* is concealed by *avidyā*, it does not mean that *Brahman* has been destroyed. One cannot say whether It exists, but one cannot also say whether It has been destroyed. It is only upon the removal of the veil of ignorance

7. Ibid.

that the knowledge of the existence or non-existence of *Brahman* may be determined. Since *avidyā* is dependent upon *Brahman,* how can it be said to have destroyed the very light/Consciousness which reveals it? And all of this is purely from an empirical (*vyāvahārika*) standpoint. From the absolute (*pāramārthika*) standpoint, there is no *avidyā* at all and *Brahman* is neither concealed nor destroyed but eternally is.

Objection 2

According to the Advaitin, *Brahman* is Consciousness. Everything other than *Brahman* is insentient. Thus there is a fundamental difference between the two. Upon the concealment of the sun by a cloud, perhaps it does not mean the sun's destruction. But the same cannot be said for *Brahman.* It is a fundamental tenet of Advaita that light and darkness, knowledge and ignorance are mutually exclusive. Thus, for *Brahman*-consciousness to be concealed is to be destroyed.

Reply 2

What is at issue, the Advaitin replies, is not the difference between a sentient *Brahman* and insentient objects. As well, one must not forget the distinction the Advaitin makes between *svarūpa-jñāna* and *vṛtti-jñāna. Brahman* as *svarūpa-jñāna* is not opposed to *avidyā.* In fact, far from being opposed to *avidyā, svarūpa-jñāna* is both ignorance's locus and that which reveals it. It is due to the presence of *Brahman*-knowledge (*svarūpa-jñāna*) that even the existence of *avidyā,* its concealment of *Brahman,* and so on, can be known and cognized.

Far from being antagonists, *svarūpa-jñāna* and *avidyā* stand in the relation of revealer and revealed. When *avidyā,* though revealed by *Brahman,* conceals It, it is said that *Brahman* is not known. When *avidyā* is removed by an impartite knowledge of the Self, it is said that *Brahman* is known. Whether it be the sun or *Brahman,* being known or not known presupposes *avidyā.* When one assumes the existence of ignorance and its power of concealment, the object is not known. When one assumes the existence of ignorance and its removal, the object is known. All these cognitions are instances of *vṛtti-jñāna.* Every instance of *vṛtti-jñāna* presupposes *svarūpa-*

jñāna and thus it is incorrect to assume *Brahman's* destruction based upon concealment.

OBJECTION 3

Rāmānuja's final objection posits that it is impossible to conceal *Brahman*-knowledge at all.

> *Ajñāna* which is the cause of the concealment of *Brahman's* nature hides *Brahman* insofar as *Brahman* is conscious of it, and on the other hand that having hidden *Brahman*, it becomes the object of consciousness on the part of *Brahman*; and this evidently involves the fallacy of mutual dependence.[8]

REPLY 3

Advaita does not hold the view that *Brahman* is conscious of *avidyā*. Rāmānuja's whole objection is based upon this fallacy. In asking whether *avidyā* first conceals *Brahman* and then becomes an object of *Brahman's* consciousness, or whether *avidyā* first becomes an object of *Brahman's* consciousness and then hides it, he has misunderstood the Advaitin's position.

According to Advaita, *avidyā* is experienced by the *jīva* and not by *Brahman*. If this is so, then the view that *Brahman*-knowledge is concealed by *avidyā* is quite tenable. Time and again we have observed that *Brahman*-as-it-is is neither witness to, nor has the experience of *avidyā*. It is *Īśvara* who knows both *avidyā* and its manifestations and it is the *jīva* who experiences the deluding power of *avidyā* and becomes its victim.

OBJECTION 4

According to Vedānta Deśika, the true nature of *Brahman* cannot be concealed or obscured by *avidyā*.[9] He asks, 'What is meant by concealment (*tirodhāna*)?' Is it: (1) the removal of the relation of the sense organs to the object? (2) the removal of the object being the content of the cognition generated by the sense organs? (3) the removal of the object being the content of all cognitions? (4) the absence of its being the object of its own knowledge? (5) the cessation of its being self-luminous? (6) the rendering indistinct of

8. *Śrī-bhāṣya* I.1.1.
9. Vide *Śatadūṣaṇī*, *Vāda* 35.

what is distinctly manifest? (7) the denial of one of the accessory factors that cause the manifestation of *Brahman*? (8) something that is indescribable?

According to the Advaitin, the first three alternatives are unacceptable since *Brahman* will never be admitted as the content of knowledge generated by the sense organs. For obvious reasons, the fourth alternative is also unacceptable.

The fifth and sixth alternatives deserve some consideration. These are virtually the same objections which Rāmānuja raised in the *Śrī-bhāṣya*. The Advaitin answers these objections in the same manner in which they replied to Rāmānuja's criticisms.

The seventh alternative is untenable according to the Advaitins because they do not attribute parts to the partless *Brahman*. And finally the last objection is untenable, according to Vedānta Deśika, because he cannot conceive of any kind of manifestation other than *Brahman* Which is immutable and indeterminate in character.

REPLY 4

According to Advaita, *tirodhāna* means the *jīva's* non-apprehension of the essential nature of *Brahman*. This in no way affects *Brahman* just as a blind individual's failure to see the sun in no way affects the sun. Without differentiating the *avidyā*-laden empirical *jīva* from *Brahman*-as-it-is, all kinds of misunderstanding arise. Śaṅkara said:

> *Brahman* is known in two forms as qualified by limiting conditions owing to the distinctions of name and form, and also as the opposite of this, i.e. as what is free from all limiting conditions whatever ... thus many (*śruti*) texts show *Brahman* in two forms according as it is known from the standpoint of *vidyā* or from that of *avidyā*.[10]

It is obvious that the Advaitin does not speak of two *Brahmans*, but of one and the same *Brahman* as seen from two different perspectives. By forgetting or ignoring this distinction, the critics of Advaita have merrily gone about their business of criticizing their own views as to what Advaita says—and not what Advaita really says.

10. *Brahma-sūtra-bhāṣya* I.1.11.

CHAPTER FOUR

THE UNTENABILITY OF AVIDYĀ'S NATURE

INTRODUCTION

Advaita's theory of Reality presents a problem which every monistic or non-dualistic system has to confront. In this case, if *Brahman* alone is real, how to account for the seeming plurality of the universe which is an experienced fact of perception? This is the philosophical problem of the One and the many—a problem upon which most systems fail.

The question as to the nature of *avidyā* receives a double analysis in Rāmānuja's *Śrī-bhāṣya.* His initial analysis of the problem begins by asking whether *avidyā* is real or unreal—what is its ontological status? This line of enquiry proceeds by attacking one of the Advaitin's chief arguments proving the illusory character of the universe—the famous syllogism which has for its probans (*hetu*) 'cognisability' or *dṛśyatva.* "The universe under dispute is illusory, because it is cognised; whatever is cognised is illusory, like the shell-silver."[1]

Rāmānuja's second objection stems from the first. After enquiring into the question of the ontological status of *avidyā*, and learning that it is neither real nor unreal (*svarūpa-anupapatti*), he continues this line of questioning and attacks the Advaitin's theory of indescribability—*anirvacanīyatā.* This becomes the fourth major objection or *anirvacanīya-anupapatti*—one which we will take up in the next chapter.

COGNIZABILITY

What is the proof that the universe is illusory? The Advaitins offer several criteria of which the most famous is their argument on cognizability. Because an object is seen, it is not unreal. Because an object is sublated, it is not real. Thus the universe of objects is

1. *Brahma-sūtra-bhāṣya, Adhyāsa-bhāṣya.*

neither real nor unreal, but illusory, *mithyā*. According to Advaita, anything which is both cognized and sublated is *mithyā*.[2]

Cognitions, by their very nature, are object-oriented. What a cognition is, is determined by the object as per the well-known dictum, 'as the object, so the cognition' (*jñeyādhīnam jñānam*). How is it then that the universe which is cognized is really but *Brahman*? Both the subject (this) and the predicate (universe) of a cognition of the universe are existent, i.e. 'this is the universe'. What is unreal is the relation between the 'this' and the 'universe'. This is supported by the *śruti* texts:

> Where one sees nothing else, hears nothing else, understands nothing else that is the Infinite. But where one sees, hears, understands something else, that is the finite.[3]

Objection 1

Vedānta Deśika submits the Advaitin's conception of *mithyā* to an examination. He asks, 'What does *mithyā* mean?' Is it: (1) unreality? (2) being the content of apprehension otherwise? (3) being different from the real as well as the unreal? (4) being the counter-correlate of the negation of what is found in a particular locus? (5) being cognized in the same locus as its own absolute non-existence? (6) being different from the real *Brahman*? or (7) something else?[4]

Advaita does not accept the first two possibilities. *Mithyā* means neither that which is totally unreal (e.g., a square circle) nor that which is the object of apprehension-otherwise (as the Bhāṭṭa-mīmāṃsakas claim).

The fourth possibility is partially correct, according to Advaita. *Mithyātva* is negated even where it is found. The water, which is found in the desert, is later sublated by the correct cognition, 'this is sand'. In a similar manner, the illusory world is later sublated by the cognition, 'this is *Brahman*'.

The critic asks, 'Is the illusoriness of the universe illusory or not?' If it is illusory, then the universe must be real. A double

2. *Śrī-śaṅkarāśaṅkara-bhāṣya-vimarśaḥ*, p. 127. *yasya pratītibādhau tadeva mithyā*. Also *Advaita-siddhi*, p. 31.
3. *Chāndogya Upaniṣad* VII.xxiv.1.
4. Vide *Śatadūṣaṇī*, *Vāda* 15 and *Tattvapradīpikā*, pp. 32-33.

negation produces a positive or, in philosophical language, this suffers from the fallacy of establishing what is already established.

On the other hand, if illusoriness is itself not illusory, then the question becomes: Is it one with *Brahman* or different from It? The former alternative reflects the Viśiṣṭādvaitin's position since the world is an organic part of *Brahman*. The latter alternative suffers from an inconclusive probans. That is, the probans is absent from that thing in which it is sought to be established. In this case, the probans is cognizability (*dṛśyatva*). In order to be a valid inference, cognizability must be invariably co-existent with illusoriness (which is the probandum of the present syllogism). But, if *mithyātva* is *Brahman* and real, and is established by cognizability, which is absent in *Brahman*, the syllogism becomes inconclusive.

Then perhaps it is the alternative positing that illusoriness is the appearance of the universe in the same locus where it does not exist at all. The water of the mirage appears in the desert, though in fact, it is not there at all.

Vedānta Deśika asks, 'How does one prove this?' Certainly perception will not suffice, for *Brahman* is not susceptible to perception. Inference proceeds only on the ground established by perception and *Scripture* does not prove it either.

Is illusoriness then something different from *Brahman*? It need not necessarily be so. A prime example is the case of the Viśiṣṭādvaitins who hold that the illusory world is different from *Brahman* —though inseparably related to It. There is even the empirical example of one rock differing from another rock. This does not establish that one of the rocks is thereby illusory.

The last alternative posits that illusoriness is 'something else'. But, if illusoriness means something, can that something be affirmed of mirage-water and negated in respect of the sand found in the desert? If this is possible, then it means that mirage-water is not illusory but sand is, a conclusion which goes directly against personal perception.

Reply 1

It is the third alternative which is the most acceptable to the Advaitin. *Mithyā* is being other than the real or the unreal (*sadasad-vilakṣaṇa*). The universe is illusory in the sense that it cannot be characterised as either real or unreal. Because it is seen, it is not unreal. Because it is sublated, it is not real. This answer will be more fully elaborated upon in the next chapter dealing with *anirvacanīyatva.*

Vedānta Deśika contends that this answer is also untenable. He says that there is no such entity which is neither real nor unreal. Either a thing is real or it is unreal. There is no middle ground between the two.

All of the other objections posed by Vedānta Deśika are based upon a confusion between Advaita's two levels of reality. What is pertinent to one level does not pertain to the other. For instance, the illusoriness of the world is itself illusory. But this does not mean that it is therefore real. The world is illusory, illusoriness is illusory. All of this pertains to the empirical level, from the *jīva's* point of view. It is the *jīva* who cognizes illusion as real. Once *Brahman*-knowledge arises, both the cognizer and the cognized disappear.

Again, the universe of illusion does not exist in *Brahman,* though it appears so as it is superimposed upon *Brahman.* In this sense, it is illusory. In actual fact, from the ultimate point of view, there is only *Brahman.*

Brahman, without undergoing any change, appears as the universe. The universe is known as the 'seen' (*dṛśya*). In this regard it cannot be unreal, for the absolutely unreal like the 'square-circle' is only words. Nor can the universe be regarded as real on its own right. It is insentient and hence depends upon *Brahman* for its being. It is in this sense that the universe is said to be neither real nor unreal.

RĀMĀNUJA'S SVARŪPA-ANUPAPATTI

Objection

Rāmānuja says, "Further, is this Nescience which makes the non-dual *Brahman* appear as manifold real or unreal?"[5] What is the nature or ontological status of *avidyā*? It must be either real or unreal since there is no third position. This argument is based on the law of excluded middle which states that anything must be either P or not-P. Judgments opposed as contradictories cannot

5. *Śrī-bhāṣya* I.1.1, p. 57.

both be false, nor can they admit the truth of a third or middle judgment, but one or the other must be true, and the truth of the one follows from the falsehood of the other. Thus, *avidyā* must either be (1) real (*paramārtha*) or (2) unreal (*aparamārtha*).

If *avidyā* is real, it leads to dualism. This position is totally unacceptable to Advaita. "It is not real since the Advaitins do not accept it."[6] As well, if it is real, then it cannot be destroyed for, according to Advaita, what is real cannot be sublated. And if it cannot be sublated, then liberation becomes impossible and the Scriptures are rendered meaningless.

On the other hand, if *avidyā* is unreal, then it must be unreal as: (1) the cognizer (*draṣṭā*); (2) or the object which is cognized (*dṛśya*); or (3) the knowledge of cognition (*dṛśi*). "Nor can it be unreal, for in that case it must be the knower, or the object known, or perception or pure Knowledge."[7]

According to Advaita, the empirical world is supported by *avidyā*. The empirical world is due to *avidyā* and is always thought of in terms of the triple forms (*tripuṭī*), i.e. the cognizer, the object cognized, and the means of cognition. Any process of knowing implies a subject who knows, an object which is known and the act of cognition thereof.

Rāmānuja says, "It cannot be knowledge, for in that case it must be either identical with or different from it."[8] If the nature of *avidyā* is identical with knowledge (*dṛśi*), then *Brahman* would be unreal. The Advaitin says that *Brahman* is one and non-dual, distinctionless and knowledge itself. If *avidyā* were identical with *Brahman*, the knowledge and ignorance would be identical and *Brahman* would be unreal. "It cannot be identical, for in that case it would be identical with *Brahman* Which is pure Knowledge and as a result, since Nescience is unreal, *Brahman* too would be unreal."[9]

Suppose the Advaitin says that knowledge (*dṛśi*) is identical with *Brahman* and unreal—he can't, but for argument's sake let us say he does, then, there is no ground (*adhiṣṭhāna*) for *avidyā*. Yet, according to Advaita, every error must have a support (*niradhiṣ*-

6. Ibid.
7. Ibid.
8. Ibid.
9. Ibid., pp. 57-58.

ṭhāna-bhrama). "Even imagined things must have something to stand upon."[10] In this case, *Brahman* is knowledge and if knowledge is unreal, then *Brahman* is unreal. This lands the Advaitin in the position of espousing Śūnyavāda—the theory of nothingness.

Rāmānuja says:

> It cannot also be non-identical, for, knowledge according to the Advaitins is non-differentiated. If Nescience is of the nature of consciousness and at the same time unreal, it would mean that we have two kinds of consciousness and this would contradict the Advaita doctrine of oneness.[11]

Thus, since the Advaitin declares that there is only one type of knowledge, either non-duality is untenable or else *Brahman* is untenable.

Suppose that the Advaitin says that knowledge (*dṛśi*) is unreal. The question becomes: What makes it unreal? There must exist an outside factor which renders it unreal.

This has the consequences of producing either circular reasoning if you say that *avidyā* is the unknown factor which makes *avidyā* unreal, or infinite regress if it is an unreal unknown factor other than *avidyā* which makes *avidyā* unreal, or a contradiction if it is a real unknown factor other than *avidyā* which makes *avidyā* unreal. In all three cases, the possibilities are untenable. Rāmānuja says:

> The unreal Nescience cannot be the knower, the object known or the perception connecting the two, for in that case there must be some other Nescience which is the cause of this unreal Nescience even as this first Nescience is the cause of the unreal world. That second Nescience must have a third Nescience which gives rise to the second and so on *ad infinitum*.[12]

If *Brahman* is said to be the cause of the unreal *avidyā*, then there is no need to posit another *avidyā* or any other unknown

10. Vide Śaṅkara's *Bhāṣya* on Gauḍapāda's *Māṇḍūkya-kārikā*.
11. *Śrī-bhāṣya* I.1.1, p. 58.
12. Ibid.

factor to be the cause. Yet, if *Brahman* is the cause, then being eternal, *avidyā* will also be eternal. This renders liberation impossible and Scripture unnecessary.

If the Advaitin says that the cognizer, the object cognized, and the resulting knowledge are all three together responsible for *avidyā*, then there arises another problem. The distinction between the knower, known, and knowledge arises due to *avidyā* and if all three are unreal, then what is responsible for *avidyā*? If everything is unreal, what makes *avidyā* rise? It cannot be an unknown factor. It can't be causeless. If the world has a cause, then this unknown factor must have a cause. Again we land in an infinite regress.

The ontological status of *avidyā* cannot be that *avidyā* does not exist and *Brahman* is the cause and locus of this non-existent defect for then, because *Brahman* is eternal, liberation becomes impossible. As well, if *Brahman* has a defect, then the defect, too, would be eternal. This would invoke the contingency of not getting liberation (*anirmokṣa-prasaṅga*).

Thus, there must be *Brahman* plus a defect called *avidyā*. If they are both real, then there is dualism. If *avidyā* is unreal, then what is its cause? For this, there will not be an answer which doesn't land in an infinite regress. Rāmānuja, on the other hand, says that *avidyā* is real and different from *Brahman*, though dependent upon It. The Advaitin counters that there is a third option open which the critic failed to offer as a valid choice. Advaita says that *avidyā* is *anirvacanīya*. This leads to the fourth major objection of Rāmānuja's entitled *anirvacanīya-anupapatti*.

Reply

The Advaitins answer this objection by stating that *avidyā* can be regarded as an object of perception (*dṛśya*). By an 'object of perception' is meant what is identified with, i.e. superimposed upon, the consciousness delimited by a mental mode (*vṛtti*). *Avidyā* fills this requirement as it is what is superimposed upon consciousness.

This conception makes *avidyā* unique for it is also what is the cause of the perception. However, the mutual dependence which is thus involved is of the logically tenable variety since *avidyā* is a beginningless power.

To demand a cause for this *avidyā* is a futile task in view of the fact that the notion of cause itself is an expression of *avidyā*. Causation is a child of its parent, *avidyā*, and so it is inapplicable to ask it of *avidyā* itself.

Māyā and Avidyā

Before we examine the next objection, I would like to make a few comments about *māyā* and *avidyā*. *Brahman*, according to the Advaitins, is neither the originating nor the transformed cause of the world. It illusorily appears as the world and is unaffected thereby. The attributes of an illusion do not affect the reality. The attributes of water do not really belong to the desert. There never was a time when water was there, nor is there water there now, nor will there ever be in the future. The desert remains in its own nature even at the very moment when it is mistaken for a body of water. The impurities which are seen in the reflection do not spoil the prototype.

Be this as it may, the world is perceived. Though Śaṅkara did not seem to make a distinction between *māyā* and *avidyā*, some post-Śaṅkara Advaitins did.[13] *Māyā* was said to be the adjunct of *Īśvara* and *avidyā*, of the *jīva*.

This difference was put forth to make the distinction that *māyā* does not delude its abode and conforms to the desires of *Īśvara* while *avidyā* deludes its abode and does not conform to the desires of the individual souls.

From an objective perspective, *māyā* is linked to *Īśvara* and the universe. From a subjective perspective, *avidyā* is connected to the individual (*jīva*). Even as *Ātman* and *Brahman* are non-different, so too, are *māyā* and *avidyā* one. It is a distinctive feature of the human being in believing that the objective being has a composition that is not foreign to the subjective being. And yet, there is an amazingly strong tendency to view what is in essence one and non-dual as if it were many. Such is the inscrutability of *avidyā/māyā*.

The Advaitin goes against everyone's natural tendency when he claims that 'ignorance' does not belong to the individual. Ignorance is an impersonal force which is superimposed upon the individual's consciousness. *Avidyā* is but one more attribute, even

13. There were not hard and fast lines on this issue and therefore both Bhāmatī and Vivaraṇa adherents are found on either side.

if the parent of all the others, viz., maleness, femaleness, fatness, thinness, stupidity, and so on.

Individual ignorance and cosmic ignorance arise together and one cannot be thought of without the other. The Advaitin is neither an out-and-out Materialist nor a Subjective Idealist. The individual is there and the world is there and both are facts of experience.

All of the 'why' questions lead us here. Why is there *avidyā*? Why does the mind mislead us? Why is there a universe of multiplicity? The problem is a fact of experience. To the mind it is a riddle, to logic it is a puzzle.

How wonderful it is:

> *Avidyā* no doubt constitutes a defect in consciousness insofar as it impedes the presentation of non-duality and gives rise to the presentation of duality; but, on the other hand, it constitutes an excellence since it forms the material cause, and thus renders possible the cognition of *Brahman*.[14]

There is a saying that by the mind one is bound and by the mind one is liberated. The individual soul is bound by the chains of ignorance, but it is also by the power of ignorance that liberation is achieved. Remember, there is a special type of ignorance called *akhaṇḍākāra-vṛtti-jñāna* which gives the liberating knowledge. Whether one calls this knowledge or ignorance, according to the Advaitin, all is *avidyā* except *Brahman*-knowledge (which is not knowledge-of but knowledge-as-it-is).

14. G.N. Jha, *Indian Thought*, vol. ii, p. 177.

CHAPTER FIVE

THE UNTENABILITY OF INEXPLICABILITY

INTRODUCTION

Earlier we observed that *māyā* can be studied from three different standpoints.[1] The ordinary day-to-day empirically engrossed individual considers the world of *māyā* to be real (*vāstavī*). The individual who is versed in the Scripture and knows *Brahman* regards the world as unreal (*tuccha*). The seekers and intellectuals who trust in their intellects maintain that *māyā* is neither real nor unreal (*anirvacanīya*).

The Advaitin regards all diversity as illusion (*mithyā*). The real (*sat*) is eternal Being, that which cannot be sublated. As *Brahman* alone fulfils this condition, It is the sole Reality. The unreal (*asat*) is that which is absolutely nothing. This world, in all its multiplicity, is neither real nor unreal. It is not real, for it suffers sublation. It is not unreal, for it is seen. The totally unreal, viz., a son of a barren woman or a square circle, has never been, nor never will be, seen. They are totally non-existent except as verbal conceptions.

The world possesses practical efficiency. As such, it is not totally non-existent. The water in the mirage is neither existent nor non-existent. Though it is psychologically given (*prasiddha*), it cannot be logically established (*pramāṇa-siddha*). This gives it a special status. The world appears, even if it eventually disappears.

Avidyā/māyā is the power of *Brahman*. It cannot really be different from *Brahman*-knowledge, since, if it were different, the scriptural texts declaring non-difference would be contradicted. Nor can it be non-different from *Brahman*, since identity is not possible between the real and the illusory, knowledge and ignorance, the sentient and the insentient. Nor can it be both different and non-

1. *Pañcadaśī* VI.130. *tucchā' nirvacanīyā ca vāstavī ce'ty asau tridhā/ jñeyā māyā tribhir bodhaiḥ śrautayauktika-laukikaiḥ//*

different, since contradictories cannot reside in one and the same location.

Avidyā/māyā cannot have parts, since if it did it would have a beginning but it is beginningless. If it had parts it would also require another entity as its cause, which would lead to infinite regress. If it was partless it could not be the cause of, and one with, the world's multiplicity. It cannot have both parts and be partless, since that is contradictory. Because of all these reasons, it is not possible to describe or determine the nature of *avidyā/māyā* in any of the human categories and thus it is called indeterminable, inexpressible, *anirvacanīya*. Its ontological status is different from both the real and the unreal (*sadasad-vilakṣaṇa*).

Avidyā/māyā cannot be something other than *Brahman* because there is no second to *Brahman*. Further, if it were, this would constitute a limit to the limitless *Brahman*. It cannot constitute the nature of *Brahman* or else it would not be known as *avidyā*. To say that *avidyā* exists is to limit *Brahman*, and yet to say that it does not exist is to fly in the face of experience and the appearance of the world will not be accounted for. It is real enough to produce the world, but not real enough to constitute a limit to *Brahman*.[2]

The totally non-existent is that which cannot exist. It is not a case of 'factual' or 'empirical' non-existence, but one of 'logical' impossibility. And, on the other hand, when the existent appears as it is not, error arises. This leaves us with three categories of existence: the existent, the appearance, and the non-existent.

What is existent can *appear* in two forms. Either it can be observed as an existent which is known as-it-is, or it can be observed as-it-is-not. Appearance is a common characteristic of these two cases of existents and thus, by itself, is not the decisive feature of the existent. What is given in experience cannot, by itself, be the criterion of validity of an experience. For validity, the ontological requirement that something must appear as-it-is is necessary. Obviously the water in the mirage does not fulfil this requirement. Hence, its existence is not valid or the same as when its appearance is cognized as sand.

The non-existent cannot appear and appearance does not prove existence. This proves that a 'mere appearance' (not appearance

2. *Brahma-sūtra-bhāṣya*, *Adhyāsa-bhāṣya*, pp. 1-3.

as-it-is, but appearance as-it-is-not) falls into a region which is neither non-existence nor existence. Sublatability is the test, though, it should be noted, that existents as given in experience are of differing sorts.

The water in a mirage is held to be less real than the mirage itself. Both existents are sublatable. The water appears and disappears even as the world of multiplicity appears and disappears. Neither entity fits the category of an eternally changeless existent.

This concept and experience of a changing existent is a riddle. To exist, by definition, is to be oneself, in one's own nature. To exist contingently is to be oneself for a certain duration of time. It is not logically impossible or self-contradictory for a contingent fact to cease to exist.

Thus, we arrive at *avidyā/māyā*. The Advaitin calls all that appears, yet is eventually sublatable, as *avidyā/māyā*. It is that which is indeterminable as either real or unreal. But just because the world has an absence of reality (meaning it is not unchanging), it does not mean that the empirical sources of knowledge, perception and the like, become invalid due to their objects being devoid of reality. Absence of reality does not render perception invalid.

We just proved that an absence of reality is not contradictory to the absence of unreality. The entire phenomenon of *avidyā/māyā* is neither real nor unreal. A two-valued logic is not applicable here. To say that the world is not real is not to say, by logical implication, that the world is real or *vice versa*. The Advaitin's conception of unreality is both a logical impossibility and an empirical impossibility, i.e. a son of a barren woman or a square circle. But the world of *avidyā/māyā* is neither logically impossible nor empirically impossible—though it may be conceptually indeterminable.

The world of *avidyā/māyā* is comprised of illusions, dreams and the world of multiplicity. Anything that is perceived or experienced is given some sort of existence. What is to be clearly understood is that the reality which is given to such objects of perception is not the reality which is given to *Brahman*. Earlier we noted that Advaita admits of three levels of reality: that which is apparently real (*prātibhāsika*), that which is empirically real (*vyāvahārika*), and that which is absolutely real (*pāramārthika*).

That which is apparently real has a reality which is very much restricted. Such existents are real to an individual at the time they are experienced. But once the earlier cognition suffers sublation, they cease to be real. Their reality is subject to given individuals at a given time. A good example to show that perceptions are possible of objects that do not necessarily exist in empirical reality is the case of dreams.

Empirical objects of one's normal waking consciousness are not as restricted as *prātibhāsika* objects. Their reality is not subject to a given individual nor a given time. Their reality is 'public' in the sense that they are experienced by more than one individual simultaneously. They also endure longer. The reality of the entire empirical world of multiplicity persists until liberation occurs. However, since even these objects suffer sublation they are not absolutely real.

RĀMĀNUJA'S ANIRVACANĪYA-ANUPAPATTI

Rāmānuja says;

> Again, the Advaitins say that Nescience (*avidyā*) is *anirvacanīya*, i.e. it is neither real nor unreal—it is unspeakable.[3]

According to Viśiṣṭādvaita, epistemology is guided by one's cognitions (*pratīti*). The minimum claim that they make is that there is such a thing as consciousness and this consciousness points towards an object. The maximum claim they make is that all knowledge is valid and there is no such thing as error. The *Śrī-bhāṣya* says:

> Those who understand the *Veda* hold that all cognition has for its object what is real; for *śruti* and *smṛti* alike teach that everything participates in the nature of everything else.[4]

The *Yatīndramatadīpikā* says:

> Since it has been said that according to the knowers of Vedānta all knowledge is of the real, the perceptual knowledge in the form of error etc. is of the real.[5]

3. *Śrī-bhāṣya,* I.1.1.
4. *Śrī-bhāṣya,* I.1.1.
5. *Yatīndramatadīpikā* I.3, p. 14.

As well, Rāmānuja contends that cognition helps to determine the nature of an object as such-and-such by employing the well-known principle, 'as the cognition, so the object' (*mānādhīnā meya-siddhiḥ*). Though, whatever the cognition, all cognitions have for their object only what is qualified by attributes. As Hiriyanna so beautifully put it, according to the Viśiṣṭādvaitins, 'the language of grammar is the language of reality'.

Viśiṣṭādvaitins hold that *Brahman*, as well as every object of one's knowledge, is qualified by attributes. Rāmānuja tried to justify this position on the ground that every valid source of knowledge (*pramāṇa*) conveys the knowledge of an object which is only qualified (*saviśeṣa*).[6]

With this in mind, Rāmānuja asks the Advaitin how he justifies his claim that *avidyā* is *anirvacanīya*. He goes further and asks, 'How do you obtain your cognition that *avidyā* is *anirvacanīya*?' All the objects in the world are either real or unreal. There is no third alternative. To claim that there is a third category of existence, as you seem determined to do, is to falsify the very basis of one's knowledge. On the basis of experience, there is no cognition (*pratīti*) which supports your claim. To say that the objects cognized in the world are *anirvacanīya* is to ignore your own experienced cognitions and to do so has the consequences of implying that anything can become the content of any cognition. If cognitions do not reveal what is experienced in them, then a cognition of a desert might in fact be a cognition of a lake, which is absurd.[7]

Post-Rāmānuja Objection 1

The critic says, 'Why don't you say that the *svarūpa* of *avidyā* is both real and unreal (*sadasat*)?' Instead of saying that *avidyā* is neither real nor unreal or, different from both real and unreal, reformulate your criterion of what is real and unreal and call it both real and unreal. Use the criteria of: what is experienced or cognized is real (*sat*) and what suffers contradiction or sublation is unreal (*asat*). Thus, since *avidyā* is experienced, it is real. Since *avidyā* is sublated, it is unreal.

6. *Śrī-bhāṣya* I.1.1. *saviśeṣavastu-viṣayatvāt sarvapramāṇānām.*
7. *Śrī-bhāṣya* I.1.1. *sadasadākārāyāḥ pratīteḥ sadasadvilakṣaṇaviṣaya ityabhyupagamyamāne sarvaṃ sarvapratīterviṣayaḥ syāt.*

REPLY 1

This argument is fallacious and untenable according to the Advaitins. Let us illustrate this with an inferential syllogism. The Viśiṣṭādvaitin claims that *avidyā* is real. This is both the statement (*pratijñā*) and the conclusion (*nigamana*). The reason or probans (*hetu*) is: Because *avidyā* is cognized. The universal proposition with example (*udāharaṇa*) is: Whatever is cognized is real, e.g., the world. The application (*upanaya*) is: *avidyā* is cognized which is invariably concomitant with what is real. Thus, the conclusion: Therefore, *avidyā is real.*

However, this argument of the Viśiṣṭādvaitin has no proving instance in support of the criterion that what is experienced or cognized is real.[8] At least, the Viśiṣṭādvaitin cannot cite one example which is acceptable to the Advaitin. The Advaitin asks the Viśiṣṭādvaitin to prove his argument with a supporting example.

Brahman cannot be said to be the example, for, *Brahman* is knowledge as-it-is, pure Consciousness, and thus neither cognized nor experienced. Pure knowledge is not an object of knowledge and can never become such.

Nor can the Viśiṣṭādvaitin cite empirical objects like sticks and stones as proving instances of his syllogism. The Advaitin maintains that empirical objects, since they are cognized, are neither real nor unreal, but are illusory. Whatever is cognized is illusory and thus, *avidyā* too, is illusory and not real.

Neither can the Viśiṣṭādvaitin claim that *avidyā* is unreal because it fits their criterion of: whatever suffers sublation is unreal. What is unreal, e.g., the son of a barren woman or a square circle, is never experienced. Therefore, the question of speaking about a sublated entity which is never cognized or presented to experience is an absurdity. Only that which is existent or presented to experience can be negated. It is necessary for a previous cognition in order to have a subsequent denial. After all, negation presupposes affirmation.

It is an accepted practice that when an example is given in an argument to prove a general proposition, that example must be

8. *Śrī-śaṅkarāśaṅkara-bhāṣya-vimarśaḥ*, p. 287. *yat sat tat pratīyate ityatra dṛṣṭāntābhāvāt.*

accepted by both the parties involved in the argument. This is a generally accepted convention and thus, when Advaita says: What is cognized is not unreal and what is sublated is not real—this conflicts with the Viśiṣṭādvaitin's position of: What is cognized is real and what is sublated is unreal.

Objection 1*a*

So, the Viśiṣṭādvaitin proposes another example which he thinks will be acceptable to the Advaitin. He proposes *Brahman* as his example, since *Brahman* includes both the major and middle terms (what is real and what is cognized).

Reply 1*a*

But, this solution too, is unacceptable to the Advaitin. *Brahman* is real (*sat*). It is true, but It is not cognized. *Brahman* is real, not because It is cognized, but because It is not sublated.

The critic replies, 'Even if this is as you say, isn't my position correct also?'

The Advaitin replies, 'No, because *Brahman* is not an object of knowledge. *Brahman* is not cognized.' To say that *Brahman* was cognized would be to make an object out of *Brahman*-knowledge. However, *Brahman* is knowledge, not an object of knowledge. Knowledge and an object of knowledge are not the same. If *Brahman* were an object of knowledge, the consequences would be: *Brahman* would be insentient; this would run contrary to Scripture. The actual position is that *Brahman* is one and non-dual. There is no one to know and nothing to be known.

Reply 1*b*

Suppose the Advaitin were to grant for the sake of argument that *Brahman* is an object of knowledge (*Brahman* isn't but suppose), then a *reductio ad absurdum* would arise. The question would become: Who is the knower of this object/*Brahman*? In any instance of knowledge, there must be a knower, a known and the act of knowledge thereof. But, since *Brahman* is one and non-dual, there is no other entity which could be this knower.

Another difficulty with this position entails the fact that *Brahman* is knowledge as-it-is. Thus, if an individual knows *Brahman* as an object, this also means that knowledge is knowing knowledge.

Knowledge of the knowledge *ad infinitum* would occur and this is the fallacy of infinite regress.

Then in what sense is *Brahman* known? According to Advaita, to be an object of knowledge requires two conditions: (1) The object must be pervaded by a mental mode (*vṛtti-vyāpya*), and (2) The object must be pervaded by knowledge (*phala-vyāpya*). If both conditions are present, then an object can be known. If both conditions are not present, then there is no object of knowledge present.

Now, in the case of knowing *Brahman*, there is a mental mode present (*vṛtti-vyāpyātva*), but there is no object of knowledge (*phala-vyāpyātva*). *Brahman* is not an object of knowledge. The mind takes the form of an impartite mode (*akhaṇḍākāra-vṛtti-jñāna*) (a mode which is formless). But since *Brahman*, which is light, Knowledge, pure Consciousness, self-revealing needs no other light to be revealed by, it is automatically revealed. It is only in this sense that *Brahman* is said to be known. However, since both conditions of knowledge are not met, *Brahman* is not an object of knowledge.

Objection 2

The critic takes up his objection in another manner. Even if the Advaitin is correct in saying that *avidyā* is different from the unreal, still, the critic maintains, *avidyā* is real. Individuals experience the world as real. In a similar manner, *avidyā* is also real. One's day-to-day empirical experience can neither be ignored nor denied.

Reply 2

According to Advaita, the claim that *avidyā* is real is untenable. Advaita makes a distinction between what is absolutely real and what is empirically or relatively real. *Brahman* alone is absolutely real because It does not suffer sublation. The empirical world of objects is only relatively real because objects exist at one time and cease to exist later on. When Advaita says that *avidyā* is not real, it means that ignorance is different from the absolutely real.

We have observed that the Advaitin admits that the empirical world, as well as *avidyā*, is experienced in the individual's day-to-day experience. By partaking of this existence, they are empirically real. Thus, the critic's objection is inappropriate because it does not take into consideration the Advaitin's distinction of levels of reality.

The Advaitin may respond to this objection in another way also. According to Advaita, *Brahman* alone is real. *Avidyā* is not real, for it has no reality or being of its own. *Avidyā* seemingly partakes of reality since it is erroneously spoken of as real in the individual's day-to-day experience. Its status is really other than what is real or unreal. It cannot be different from *Brahman*—or else Advaita's non-dualism would be compromised. Scripture denies dualism. It also cannot be identical with *Brahman* because *Brahman* is sentient and *avidyā* is insentient. Thus, they are contraries like light and darkness. Nor can *avidyā* be a composite entity made up of parts—being uncaused itself. Nor can it be devoid of parts as it is the cause of composite things.

All of these arguments go to show that *avidyā* cannot be determined to be either real or unreal. It defies all the categories known to thought. Therefore, it is said to be indeterminable (*anirvacanīya*).

Chapter Six

IGNORANCE CANNOT BE POSITIVE

Introduction

It is the contention of the Viśiṣṭādvaitins that Advaita's theory of *avidyā* does not have the support of any valid means of knowledge (*pramāṇa*). This much the Advaitin also accepts. However, Advaita contends that *avidyā* is positive (*bhāva-rūpa*).[1] The implication of this is that ignorance is not a mere absence of knowledge (*jñāna-abhāva*), a negative concept (as Viśiṣṭādvaita contends), but a positive entity which is ultimately sublated by right knowledge.

Avidyā is given (*prasiddha*) but not established (*pramāṇa-siddha*). Since *Brahman* is *svarūpa-jñāna,* by Its very nature It is not opposed to ignorance. Empirical knowledge on the other hand, arises through *vṛtti-jñāna* which is, by its very nature, opposed to ignorance. Thus, no empirical knowledge known through a *pramāṇa* can illumine *avidyā*—for the two are opposed to each other. Sureśvara says:

> He who desires to see *avidyā* through the knowledge generated by a *pramāṇa* could as well certainly see the darkness in the interior of a cave by means of a lamp.[2]

Moreover, *avidyā* cannot be the object of a valid means of knowledge, for, a valid means of knowledge is that which makes known what was not already known.[3] 'What is not already known' is but another name for what is characterized by *avidyā*. If one were to admit a *pramāṇa* for the existence of *avidyā*, then one must also admit that *avidyā* is characterized by another *avidyā*, and so on *ad infinitum*.

1. Vide *Brahma-siddhi*, *Iṣṭa-siddhi*, and *Naiṣkarmya-siddhi.*
2. *Taittirīya-upaniṣad-bhāṣya-vārttika* II.177, p. 155. Also *Iṣṭa-siddhi*, I.9, p. 62.
3. *Vedānta-paribhāṣā* I, p. 5; *Iṣṭa-siddhi* I, p. 61.

Though ignorance is not established by any *pramāṇa*, it is directly manifested by the witness self (*sākṣin*).[4] Earlier we observed that the Advaitin says that the relation between *Brahman* and *avidyā* is inexplicable. It is only at the empirical level, which is itself a state of *avidyā*, that one may speak of *avidyā*. Where there is *Brahman*, there is no *avidyā*. And if *Brahman* is not known, how can one possibly speak of knowing *avidyā*, which is located in *Brahman*? As is said:

> When *Brahman* is not known through valid cognition, that there is nescience is unintelligible; and more so, when It is known; there is no unsublated false cognition. He who is endowed with nescience cannot establish it; in consideration of the nature of reality it is established that there is no nescience.[5]

Thus, *avidyā* is established by direct experience (*anubhava*). This experience is witnessed by the *sākṣin*. And whatever entity is directly manifested to the *sākṣin* does not require any proof for its existence. *Avidyā* is mysterious and inscrutable. "*Avidyā* does not stand the scrutiny of a *Pramāṇa*."[6] "Therefore, it is impossible to demonstrate through means of valid cognition that nescience is (in *Brahman*), or as of what form it is, or whence, for there is only experience (of it)."[7]

Two Powers

Advaita claims that *avidyā* is positive because it obscures or veils (*āvaraṇa*) *Brahman* and projects (*vikṣepa*) the illusory world of duality. However, in labelling *avidyā* as positive, the Advaitin does not mean to imply that it is real. He only means to convey that ignorance is something existent, and not negative.

Sometimes *avidyā* is spoken of in terms of 'non-apprehension' (*agrahaṇa*). "*Avidyā* does not consist in anything other than the

4. *Taittirīya-upaniṣad-bhāṣya-vārttika* II.438, p. 292. *na jānāmi iti sākṣi-pratītisiddham anīrvācyam ajñānam. Advaita-siddhi*, p. 575; *sā ca avidyā sākṣi-vedyā. Siddhāntabindu*, p. 189.
5. *Sambandhavārttika*, pp. 178-80.
6. Ibid., pp. 181-82.
7. Ibid., pp. 184-85.

non-perception of the Self."[8] Or again, "Non-perception (appears in the form) 'I do not know' ".[9] According to Advaita, *agrahaṇa* is an aspect of ignorance which remains even in the deep sleep state, though in a latent form. Generally it is held to be negative.

However, it is wrong to conclude from this that Advaita views *avidyā* as negative or as an absence of knowledge. There is non-perception (*agrahaṇa*) of *Brahman* because of the concealing power of *avidyā*. Concealment must be positive as it cannot be done by a negative, i.e. non-existent, entity. Instead of defining *avidyā* as an absence of knowledge, it would be more accurate to describe it as something other than knowledge.

Avidyā as Cause of the World

The cause is that which, when present, will produce the effect. We have observed that it is the existent alone which can be the cause of something. Whatever is non-existent cannot be the cause of an existent. Something cannot come out of nothing. It is by employing this type of reasoning that the Advaitins say that *avidyā*, which is the cause of the materialistic universe, must be something existent and therefore positive.

However, it must be kept in mind that, even though *avidyā* is the cause of the world of multiplicity, both *avidyā* and the world are neither real nor unreal. As well, merely because ignorance is positive, it does not make it real. Eventually *avidyā* must suffer sublation.

The upshot of this contention is that something existent and illusory (the world) is produced by something existent and illusory (*avidyā*) through a modification of the latter. The world-creation is an illusory product of *avidyā*. The world is not created. It is the way in which *Brahman* appears under the conditions of space, time, and other limiting adjuncts. Thus, while *avidyā* is said to be the transformative material cause of the world, *Brahman* is held to be its transfigurative material cause.

8. *Taittirīya-upaniṣad-bhāṣya-vārttika*, Brahmavallī, 179, p. 156. *ātmāgrahātirekeṇa tasyā rūpaṁ na vidyate.*
9. Ibid., Brahmavallī, 180, p. 157. *tasmātsadasadityādivikalpo mūḍhacetasām/ nirūpyamāṇo nirvati na vedmītyagrahātmani//*

Objection 1

Rāmānuja contends the Advaitin's view that an illusory object must have an illusory material cause. According to Rāmānuja, *Brahman* is both the material and the efficient cause of the world.[10] The entire world of sentient and insentient beings constitutes the body of *Brahman*. In the causal state, both *cit* and *acit* are in a subtle form. In the effect state, both *cit* and *acit* are in a gross form. This means that *Brahman* with *cit* and *acit* remaining in the subtle form is the cause of the world and *Brahman* with *cit* and *acit* in their gross form is the effect.[11]

Thus, *Brahman* as the material cause of the world, is not subject to change. Nor do the imperfections of the world belong to, or affect, *Brahman*.[12] The changes of the world belong to *acit* and the imperfections to *cit*—thereby rendering *Brahman* free from change or imperfection.

Reply 1

Rāmānuja's objection, that an object which is illusory must have as its material cause something illusory, is based upon the *Brahma-sūtra* passage:

> (*Brahman* is) not (the cause of the world) because this (world) is of a contrary nature (to *Brahman*); and its being so (i.e. different from *Brahman*) (is known) from scriptures.[13]

However, Advaita contends that this passage shows that *Brahman*, though of a nature different from the world, can nevertheless be its cause. The cause and its effect cannot be exactly similar in all respects.[14] If they were, they wouldn't be causal correlates. There must be something in the cause which is also found in the effect—thus linking them. There must also be something different in the cause distinguishing it from the effect. In a similar manner, *Brahman*, the effect, shares such qualities as 'existence' and

10. *Śrī-bhāṣya* I.4.23, pp. 202-03.
11. Rāmānuja, *Vedārthasaṅgraha*, p. 31.
12. *Śrī-bhāṣya* II.1.15.
13. *Brahma-sūtra* II.1.4. *na vilakṣaṇatvādasya tathātvaṃ ca śabdāt.*
14. *Brahma-sūtra-bhāṣya* II.1.6.

'intelligence' with the world, the effect. There are also differences between *Brahman* and the things of the world.[15]

Brahman is both the efficient and material cause of the world. But this *Brahman* is not *Brahman*-as-it-is, which is one and non-dual, non-relational and undifferentiated (*nirguṇa*).[16] It is *Brahman* as associated with *avidyā* that is the cause of the world. As such, *avidyā*, which is illusory is the material cause of the world which is also illusory.

The immutable *nirguṇa Brahman*, Which is the locus of *avidyā*, is said to be the transfigurative material cause of the world, according to Advaita. As well, it is *avidyā* in a false association with *Brahman*, which undergoes modification and is the transformative material cause of the world. Both *Brahman* and *avidyā* are necessary in order to account for this appearance of the world. *Brahman* serves as the unchanging and unaffected locus and *avidyā* serves as the changing cause. *Avidyā* transforms into the world which reveals that aspect of the material cause which is found in its effect, i.e. illusoriness and sublatability.

The relation between *Brahman* and the world is one of transfiguration or apparent change (*vivarta*). The relation between *avidyā* and the world is one of transformation or actual change (*pariṇāma*). These two are necessary in order to effect the causal chain. *Brahman*-as-it-is cannot be the cause or effect of anything. *Avidyā*-by-itself is insentient and cannot cause anything without an association with sentience.

The critic's objection that *śruti* texts ascribe causality to *Brahman* misunderstands that this causality pertains, not to the *nirguṇa Brahman*, but to *Brahman* in association with *avidyā*. The similarity found between *Brahman* and the world also pertains to this *saguṇa Brahman* and the world. Any similarity between cause and effect, *Brahman* and the world, as is alluded to in *sūtra* II.1.4, pertains to this *saguṇa Brahman*.

According to Advaita, *avidyā's* ontological status is neither real nor unreal. It is cognized so it cannot be unreal. It suffers sublation so it cannot be real. For this reason *avidyā* is called illusory (*mithyā*). Even as the transformative material cause of a gold-ring is gold, so is the transformative material cause of the illusory

15. Ibid.
16. *Śvetāśvatara Upaniṣad* VI.8. *na tasya kāryaṃ karaṇaṃ ca vidyate.*

world also illusory. This transformative material cause is *avidyā*.

Thus, Rāmānuja's objection to the Advaitin's view that the material cause of an illusory object must also be illusory is untenable.

Objection 2

Vedānta Deśika takes up the Viśiṣṭādvaitin's objection against the Advaita doctrine of *avidyā* and claims that, at best, *Brahman* is the efficient cause of the world—but not the material cause (except by courtesy). He says:

> Though that which is qualified is the material cause, the attribute alone is subject to modification. Since the entity qualified by the attribute is indirectly the locus (for the change), objection cannot be raised for the use of the word "material cause" (*upādāna*) with regard to that entity. Just as even for you (i.e. the Advaitin), though *avidyā* alone is what is subject to modification (*pariṇāma*) directly, *Brahman* is said to undergo apparent change in view of the fact that *avidyā* is dependent on the Witness—*Brahman*, even so, (in our view) though the substance (*prakṛti*) which constitutes the body of *Brahman* is subject to modification directly, *Brahman*, Which is responsible for originating the change and on Which the changing entity is dependent, can be spoken of as what is subject to change.[17]

One point before we continue this objection is that Vedānta Deśika, in stating the Advaitin's position, has used the expression '*vivarta*' and not '*pariṇāma*' with regard to their doctrine of *avidyā*. This is an incorrect account of the Advaitin's view.

Thus, according to Vedānta Deśika, the Advaitin's immutable *nirguṇa Brahman* cannot directly be the material cause of the world. At best, causality can be ascribed to *Brahman* in an indirect manner, because it is *prakṛti*, which is *Brahman's* attribute, which undergoes modification. The Viśiṣṭādvaitin's position is clear here.

Reply 2

Advaita does not say that *prakṛti* is *Brahman's* attribute. It directly posits that *Brahman*, as the unchanging locus for the world's appearance, is the direct transfigurative material cause of

17. *Śatadūṣaṇī, brahmopādānatvānyathānupapattibhaṅgaḥ.*

the world. *Brahman* does not need the agency of *prakṛti*. *Brahman* through *vivarta* and *avidyā* through *pariṇāma* are the material cause of the world. Thus, it is untenable to say that the causality of the world is due to a qualified relation between *Brahman* and *prakṛti/acit*.

To ascribe material causality to *Brahman* indirectly, as the Viśiṣṭādvaitins do would invoke the following difficulties. If *Brahman* is said to undergo change, then this conflicts with the *śruti* texts which say that *Brahman* is free from change. If *Brahman* does not undergo change, and that change really takes place in *prakṛti* (*Brahman's* body), the negation of change in *Brahman* will be unintelligible. To deny something, that something must first be affirmed. Denial of change in *Brahman* presupposes a prior affirmation of it in *Brahman*. If the change really takes place in *prakṛti*, then it will not be possible to explain the change in *Brahman*.

Advaita does not face this difficulty. The change that takes place in *avidyā* is but a false superimposition upon *Brahman* Which is its locus. The *śruti* text comes into play by negating this wrongly affirmed appearance on *Brahman* and affirming that no change takes place in *Brahman*, in actuality.

Objection 3

Vedānta Deśika contends that the cause (*māyā*) must be real. His argument basically takes the form of: the world must have a cause; the world is real, so the cause of the world must be real; *māyā*, being the cause of the world, therefore, must also be real. He says:

> The illusoriness of *māyā* would be contradicted by the absurdity which arises if *māyā* were not the cause (of the world). And the reality of the cause is quite frequently shown by examples such as clay ... The word *māyā* refers to the entity which is the instrument (*upakaraṇa*) to the creation of variegated things.[18]

Reply 3

The problem with this objection raised by Vedānta Deśika is that an instrument (*upakaraṇa*) is not the same thing as a material

18. Ibid., *māyopādānatvānyathānupapattibhaṅgaḥ*.

cause (*upādāna*). Advaita says that *avidyā* is the transformative material cause of the world even as clay is the material cause of a pot. The instruments for producing a pot are, not the clay, but the wheel and a staff.

Now, Vedānta Deśika's argument given above begins by stating that *māyā* is the material cause and ends by saying that *māyā* is the instrument for the creation of the world. But, the transformative material cause and the instrumental cause are not the same thing. Thus, the argument commits the fallacy of disharmony between the beginning and end of the statement.

The next point of disagreement between Vedānta Deśika and the Advaitins regards their views concerning the ontological status of *avidyā*. Advaita says that it is neither real nor unreal because, though perceived, it is sublatable.

Thirdly, though the Advaitins agree with Vedānta Deśika that *avidyā* is the cause of the world, they do not believe that it necessarily follows that *avidyā* is therefore real.

One final note on this argument concerns the Advaitin's position on the ontological status of a cause and its effect. Regarding the material cause, if the situation is one of transformation (*pariṇāma*), then the cause and its effect must have the same ontological status. But in the case of a transfiguration (*vivarta*), their ontological status is different—with the cause having a higher reality and the effect a lower reality. For example, in the former case, both the clay and the pot are empirically real. In the latter example, the desert is empirically real (*vyāvahārika*) and the mirage is phenomenally real (*prātibhāsika*).

According to Advaita, the relation between *avidyā* and the world is one of transformation or *pariṇāma*. Thus, the two must have the same ontological status.

Terminable

Advaita has said that *avidyā* is positive because it: (1) possesses the two powers of concealment and projection, and (2) is the transfigurative material cause of the world. A third characteristic of *avidyā* is advanced to show that it is positive. *Avidyā* is terminable (*jñāna-nivartya*).[19] The non-existent cannot be removed simply

19. *Brahma-sūtra-bhāṣya, Adhyāsa-bhāṣya*, p. 2.

because it is not. What is not has no need of removal and yet, since *avidyā* is existent and therefore something, it possesses the ability to be sublated. Since this facet of *avidyā* comprises Rāmānuja's next major objection, we will take it up in the next chapter.

Different From Prior Non-Existence

The fourth reason advanced by the Advaitins saying that *avidyā* is positive is that *avidyā* is different from a prior non-existence of knowledge (*jñāna-prāgabhāva*). If *avidyā* were merely an absence of knowledge, it would be a negative entity. But it is not just an absence of knowledge, according to Advaita. This aspect will be further developed when we analyse the Advaitin's position regarding perception (which immediately follows).

Perception

The Advaitins assert that perception, inference, verbal testimony, and implication all help to establish that *avidyā* is positive. *Avidyā* cannot be established by any *pramāṇa.* Advaita accepts this, and yet, they advance several points which help to render the doctrine of a positive *avidyā* meaningful.[20]

Individuals experience ignorance of a multitude of things. Everyone has a direct experience of this in the form 'I am ignorant'. This perceptual experience is technically known as '*sākṣi-pratyakṣa*'. As such, it is suggestive of the existence of *avidyā.* And, aided by reasoning, it demonstrates that *avidyā* is positive.

The question arises: Is this *avidyā* a positive conception or is it a mere absence of knowledge? According to Advaita, it cannot refer to an absence of knowledge because in the experience, 'I do not know', the experient is manifest in the form of 'I'. Everything can be doubted or denied except the 'I'. No one is able to say, 'I do not exist', without a contradiction. The very denial is but an affirmation—thus, there is not a total absence of knowledge.

20. Vide *Śrī-bhāṣya* I.1.1, pp. 61-62. For Advaita's texts for perception see *Advaita-siddhi*, pp. 548, 550; *Tattvaprakāśikā*, p. 59. For inference see *Vivaraṇa-prameya-saṅgraha*, p. 13. For implication see *Vivaraṇa-prameya-saṅgraha*, p. 20. For *śruti* see *Ṛg-veda* X.129.3; *Chāndogya Upaniṣad* VIII.2.3; *Śvetāśvatara Upaniṣad* I.3 and IV.5.

Nor can it refer to the absence of knowledge of a particular thing. Negation presupposes the knowledge of the thing negated. In order to negate a particular thing, there must first exist knowledge of the knowledge of that particular thing which is being negated. How can one have that knowledge and, at the same time, have its negation?[21]

The contention is that knowledge cannot know its absence because the two are incompatible. One cannot know that something is not, unless one first has the knowledge of its presence.

As well, there is the evidence provided by the deep-sleep state to demonstrate that *avidyā* is positive. Upon waking, an individual states that they have slept well. At the same time, they state that they knew nothing while asleep. Such a recollection presupposes a prior experience. When an individual states that they were ignorant while they were asleep, it means that they had at that time, the experience or knowledge of ignorance.

Rāmānuja's Objection 1

Rāmānuja contends that perception does not demonstrate that *avidyā* is positive either at the waking, dreaming, or deep-sleep state. It shows only an absence of knowledge and nothing positive. He says:

> All this is untenable. In the perception 'I am ignorant; I do not know myself', Nescience is not perceived as a positive entity. The defects shown with respect to Nescience being non-knowledge equally apply to Nescience taken as a positive entity and not a mere negation of knowledge.[22]

Thus, *avidyā* is merely a negative entity.

Reply 1

The Advaitin contends that whenever one has knowledge of a negative entity, two conditions must be fulfilled. One must know: (1) the object which is absent (*pratiyogin*), and (2) the place where the object is absent (*anuyogin*). It is meaningless to talk of a mere

21. Vide *Advaita-siddhi* p. 555. Also vide *Pañcapādikā-vivaraṇa*, pp. 74-75. *aham ajñaḥ iti jñānasya...abhāvavilakṣaṇa-viṣayatvaṃ siddham.*
22. *Śrī-bhāṣya* I.1.1, p. 62.

absence of an entity alone. One should speak of the absence of something—both what it is and where it is. For example, to speak of the absence of knowledge in deep-sleep, what is required is the knowledge of both the locus and the correlate. In the state of deep-sleep, an individual cannot have the knowledge of both the locus and the correlate because the mind is quiescent at that time. And if the mind were not quiescent and the individual had the knowledge of both the *pratiyogin* and *anuyogin*, then it would not be the state of deep-sleep.[23]

The critic may object that the *pratiyogin* is knowledge and the *anuyogin* is the individual. Thus, at the time of deep-sleep, knowledge is absent in the individual. But knowledge isn't absent, according to the Advaitin. There is the knowledge that knowledge is absent. Thus, the correlate is positively known.

The critic may reply, 'How can knowledge and ignorance—which are opposed to each other, like light and darkness, co-exist in the same locus? If knowledge is positive, then ignorance must be negative.'[24]

The Advaitin asks the critic, 'Then what about your doctrine of *cidacid-viśiṣṭādvaita*? Is *acit* the opposite of *cit*? Is it *cit's* absence? Are they contradictories? If so, then how can you maintain that they constitute the body of *Brahman*?' In any event, the Advaitin does not say that *svarūpa-jñāna*, which constitutes the essential nature of *Brahman* and which is the locus of, and reveals, *avidyā*, is opposed to it. His (*Advaitin's*) position is that in deep-sleep there is *avidyā* as well as *avidyā-vṛtti*. Ignorance, which is the adjunct of the Self in deep-sleep, is the causal condition of the mind. It is through *avidyā-vṛtti* that the Self experiences ignorance in the state of deep-sleep.

The Advaitin further asks the Viśiṣṭādvaitin, 'Whom are you speaking with anyway?' and reminds, 'We are not Naiyāyikas who accept negative entities.' In fact, the Advaitin does not really accept any positive entities either. Only *Brahman* exists. It is only from the relative empirical level that the Advaitin speaks of positive and negative entities. But the reality of the situation is that this is all pure discursive imagination. *Brahman* is *ekam eva advitīyam*—one without a second.

23. Vide *Naiṣkarmya-siddhi* III.7, Jñānottama's commentary.
24. *Śrī-bhāṣya* I.1.1, p. 64.

In fact, the Viśiṣṭādvaitins, themselves, are not proponents of the negative either. They accept the doctrine of *satkāryavāda* which posits that the effect is similar to the cause. Since *Brahman*, *cit* and *acit* are all real, all their effects will also be real. The maximum claim of the Viśiṣṭādvaitin is that there is no such thing as error at all. *Brahman-cid-acit* are all real, positive, and eternal.

Again, the Advaitin says that there can never be a perceptual experience of a prior absence of knowledge. At best, it is something that must be inferred from the knowledge which takes place subsequently. That is, whenever knowledge arises, it implies that there was a prior ignorance. On the other hand, *avidyā* can be experienced directly, as we have already observed. Thus, *avidyā* must be different from a prior absence of knowledge.

The Viśiṣṭādvaitin makes a final objection: Even if we are to grant for the sake of argument (we don't, but suppose) that *avidyā* is positive, even then this will not help the Advaitin. Why? According to the Advaitin, *avidyā* is understood only in relation. That is, there is an expectancy inherent in the term itself (ignorant of what?). Thus, it follows that ignorance can be known as either: (1) absence of knowledge (*jñāna-abhāva*); (2) what is different from knowledge (*jñānād-anyaḥ*); or (3) what is opposed to knowledge (*jñāna-virodhi*).[25]

The Advaitin eliminates option number one himself. And the options number two and three are meaningful only in relation to a reference to knowledge. In a similar manner, darkness is meaningful only in relation to light. Therefore, whether *avidyā* is positive or negative, it can be known only in relation to knowledge. You yourself say that knowledge is positive. What is ignorance but knowledge (*jñāna*) plus the prefix 'not' ('*a*' or '*a*'+ '*jñāna*')? The negative prefix 'not' clinches the definition of *avidyā* as negative.

Rāmānuja's contention that the direct perception, 'I am ignorant', denotes only the prior negation of knowledge is untenable, according to Advaita. He contends that in such a perception, either *Brahman* illumines or It does not. If It does, then ignorance must vanish in its light. If It does not, then how can ignorance be known without sentience?

25. *Śrī-bhāṣya* I.1.1, p. 63.

It does not overcome the problem to contend that *Brahman* somehow partly or vaguely shines and thus is both the locus and the object of a positive ignorance. If this position were accepted, it could also be applied to the position that a prior negation of knowledge alone is involved in the perception of *avidyā*.

Nor can the problem be overcome by stating that the prior negation of knowledge abides in *Brahman*, but is indistinctly perceived—while its correlate is but a memory perception.

Advaita claims that these objections of Rāmānuja are untenable. Rāmānuja has made a mistake in stating that prior negation is a category acceptable to the Advaitin. In saying, 'the pot will come into being', what is experienced is not the prior negation of the pot, but only its present non-existence. If the pot were not real, how could it come into existence at any time?

A memory perception of absence is not an example of direct perception. It is precisely for this reason that Advaita accepts non-cognition (*anupalabdhi*) as the sixth valid means of knowledge (*pramāṇa*).

Therefore, the cognition 'I am ignorant', understood as a prior negation of knowledge, cannot become an object of perception. This apprehension must be treated as revealing a positive *avidyā*.

Vedānta Deśika also examines the Advaita position that perception demonstrates that *avidyā* is positive. His contention is that if ignorance is a positive entity known by perception, then does this ignorance manifest itself to the perceptual cognition in opposition to it, or as unopposed to it?[26]

If the perception of ignorance is opposed to ignorance itself, then the contradiction arises that the two entities are contradictory. If knowledge and ignorance are opposed to each other, then the cognition of ignorance obviously presupposes the knowledge of its opposite, viz. knowledge itself. If that knowledge is known, then the ignorance which is opposed to it would cease to exist. This would render the cognition of ignorance impossible.

On the other hand, if the perception of ignorance is not opposed to knowledge, then this flies in the face of everyone's experience. Such judgments as, 'I am ignorant', imply the negative character of ignorance.

26. *Śatadūṣaṇī*, *Vāda* 39.

Inference

According to Advaita, inference also goes to demonstrate that *avidyā* is positive. The inference is:

> All knowledge established by one of the *pramāṇas* (which is held in dispute) is preceded by something else which is different from the prior non-existence of knowledge, which obscures the object of knowledge and which exists in the same place as knowledge; because knowledge possesses the property of manifesting things not illumined before, just as the light of a lamp lit in the dark place manifests things.[27]

This inference is intended to demonstrate that all knowledge is preceded by a positive state of ignorance.

The syllogism is qualified by the following points. *Avidyā*, which is the object, is different from the absence of knowledge; it conceals its object; it is what is removed by knowledge; and it exists in the place where knowledge now exists. The syllogism itself is: *Pratijñā*—a cognition which arises through a *pramāṇa* is preceded by some positive entity. *Hetu*—the object which is not known is made known. *Udāharaṇa*—in every case of cognition there is *avidyā*, like the light of a lamp coming into the room for the first time. *Upanaya*—a cognition which is not known and is made known is invariably concomitant with a positive entity. *Nigamana*—therefore, a cognition which arises through a *pramāṇa* is preceded by some positive entity.

To word this another way, when valid knowledge arises with reference to an object, it gives rise to the cognition that this object exists. From this one can infer that prior to the rise of the valid knowledge of the object, there existed some factor in that object which gave rise to such usages as, 'the object does not exist'. This usage is removed by valid knowledge. And that factor must be different from the antecedent negation of valid knowledge. In other words, knowledge, being of the nature of the annihilation of its antecedent negation, cannot be the cause of the annihilation of its antecedent negation.[28]

27. Ibid. See also *Vivaraṇa-prameya-saṅgraha*, p. 13.
28. Vide *Advaita-siddhi*, p. 562. *vivādapadaṃ pramāṇajñānaṃ svaprāgabhāva-*

RĀMĀNUJA'S OBJECTION 1

Rāmānuja says:

> Again, in the inference that was made it was proved, rather it was attempted to prove, that the Nescience which is a positive entity rests in *Brahman* and covers It and is later destroyed by true knowledge.[29]

Rāmānuja's main objection is that the inference which is supposed to establish a positive *avidyā*, must itself be concealed in a further and different positive ignorance. If this is the case, then it follows that the original *avidyā* would not be revealed by the *sākṣin* and thus would not be removable by *Brahman*-knowledge.

Rāmānuja contends that the reason (*hetu*) is defective in the Advaitin's syllogism. He says that it is contradictory. It proves something other than what it sets out to prove. The Advaitin claims that *avidyā* is one and that it conceals *Brahman*. But the Advaitin's argument only proves that *avidyā* is concealed and not *Brahman*. And if it is the case that *avidyā* is concealed, what conceals it—another *avidyā*?

In the *hetu* what is meant by the term 'illumination'? It may be resolved into one of six alternatives: (1) being knowledge; (2) being the distinctive cause of knowledge; (3) being an aid to the sense organs; (4) being merely the cause of knowledge; (5) being the cause of the manifestation; or (6) being in a general way the cause of the empirical usage about the object either directly or indirectly.

It cannot be the first, because the reason would be defective in light of the illustration since the light of the lamp is not knowledge. It cannot be the second or the third because the reason would not be present in the subject of the syllogism. It cannot be the fourth, because there is an inconclusiveness of the reason in regard to the sense organs. It cannot be the fifth, because the reason is defective in respect of the illustration. Nor can it be the sixth alternative, since this suffers the same fate as the fifth alternative.

---

vyatirikta-svaviṣayāvaraṇa-svanivartya-svadeśagata-vastvantarapūrvakam aprakāśitārtha-prakāśakatvādandhakāre prathamotpanna-pradīpaprabhā-vat. Saṃkṣepaśārīraka III.111, p. 564.

29. *Śrī-bhāṣya* I.1.1, p. 67.

As well, the example that the Advaitin gives is just plain silly, according to Rāmānuja. In a kitchen smoke and fire co-exist. Yet, your example does not contain both the thesis and the reason. According to Rāmānuja, the Advaitin's example is missing the *hetu*. 'It makes known what is not known earlier', and this refers only to knowledge and not to ignorance.

Regarding the example, Rāmānuja says that light itself does not give knowledge. It is merely one factor among many. Though, it is true that only knowledge, given the appropriate and necessary conditions, can reveal anything.

Thus, Rāmānuja offers a counter argument. He says that *avidyā* is not destroyed by knowledge. Why? Because it is positive. Anything that is positive cannot be destroyed by knowledge, i.e. like a pot.

Reply 1

The Advaitin responds to Rāmānuja by saying that his objections rest on a misunderstanding. The inference in question is not meant to establish *avidyā* as a positive entity. That has already been done by the direct *sākṣi* perception. What the inference does is to give meaningfulness and intelligibility to the positiveness and sublatability of ignorance. Both the positiveness and sublatability of ignorance are concealed by ignorance and this veil is removed by the inference.

Scripture

The Advaitin's claim that there are *śruti* texts which state that the true nature of *Brahman* is veiled by *avidyā*. Since the non-existent or negative cannot veil an object, and since *avidyā* veils *Brahman*, it follows that *avidyā* is not a mere negation of knowledge—but a positive entity. For instance, there are texts which say:

> The true nature of *Brahman* is concealed from the individual souls by falsity.
>
> The true nature of *Brahman* is veiled from the individual souls by an entity similar to mist.[30]

30. *Taittirīya Saṃhitā* IV.vi.ii.2.

RĀMĀNUJA'S OBJECTION 1

Rāmānuja interprets the *śruti* texts differently from Advaita. He says:

> The Nescience of the Advaitins which is neither real nor unreal is not based on scriptural authority. In the text, 'These which are true are covered by what is untrue (*anṛta*)' quoted by the Advaitins, the word 'untrue' does not mean unreal or indefinable but is the opposite of what is meant by the word *ṛta* (true) and *ṛta* means such actions as do not result in any worldly enjoyment but are helpful only to attain the Lord.[31]

Rāmānuja argues that the *Chāndogya* text means that *anṛta* means action (*karma*) which is done selfishly. *Anṛta* means that action which is different from *ṛta*. The term *ṛta* means actions which are done with an attitude of propitiating God and thus enabling the devotee to attain liberation. *Anṛta* actions are those which aim at worldly results and which thus stand in the way of liberation. Thus, *anṛta* does not mean, as the Advaitin contends, what is inexplicable and what covers—and that since 'falsehood' covers or conceals something, it is therefore a positive entity.

Regarding the *Nāsadīya-sūkta* which says, "In the beginning, before creation, there was neither the real (*sat*) nor the unreal (*asat*)",[32] Rāmānuja contends that this does not show that *avidyā* was in the beginning. What it shows is a referral to the state of *pralaya* or dissolution before creation began.

Likewise in the text, "The Lord, the *Māyin*, creates through *Māyā* this world and the souls are bound in it by this *Māyā*",[33] the word '*māyā*' refers to *prakṛti* and this *māyā* is the Lord's wonderful power which He possesses, as well as the cause of the world.[34] It does not mean, as the Advaitin says, that an inexplicable *avidyā* is the source of the world and that this ignorance is a positive entity. The world (*acit*) is real and as the effect of a cause, this cause (*māyā*) must also be real. Thus ignorance is not 'neither real nor unreal'.

31. *Śrī-bhāṣya* I.1.1, p. 72.
32. *Ṛg Veda* X.129.
33. *Śvetāśvatara Upaniṣad* IV.9.
34. *Śrī-bhāṣya* I.1.1, p. 73.

The *śruti* text, "The Lord became many by His *Māyā*"[35] shows that *māyā* is a mysterious power and not *mithyā*. It refers to that which produces wonderful effects.[36]

Reply 1

According to Rāmānuja, the creation of the world is as real as *Brahman. Prakṛti* is *Brahman's* power and the creation of the universe is no more than a matter of sport for *Brahman/Īśvara. Īśvara* is described as a magician by Rāmānuja and His ability to create the universe is due to His astonishing power. In this way, Rāmānuja's description of *prakṛti*/world differs from the Advaitin's concept of *māyā*.

According to Advaita, *māyā* is indeterminate—being neither real nor unreal. *Māyā* is the power of *Īśvara*, though it is merely His wish or desire and does not exist in Him in seed form. It is the principle which makes the phenomenal appearance of the world. However, it has significance only from the empirical point of view. *Māyā* is that which (*yā*) is not (*mā*)—yet, it appears as an inscrutable power of God which veils the true and projects the false. Any attempt to enquire into it in order to render it intelligible is doomed to failure. Any enquiry made into it should only be for the purpose of transcending it. Once one is beyond it, it no longer remains a mystery and puzzle. It never was, nor will it ever be. *Brahman* alone is. Ignorance is the fact which defies all explanations. It is the explanation which says that all explanations are impossible.

Presumption

In addition to perception, inference, and Scripture demonstrating that *avidyā* is positive, presumption (*arthāpatti*) also aided by reason, does so. This is indicated by the fact that the individual is not manifest in its true nature of infinite bliss. A common definition of *Brahman* is: *saccidānanda*. If there were no ignorance obstructing this nature, it would be manifesting itself. The non-manifestation of this bliss presumptively implies that it is veiled by a factor which must be positive in nature.[37]

35. *Bṛhadāraṇyaka Upaniṣad* 4.6.19.
36. *Śrī-bhāṣya* I.1.1, p. 73.
37. *Advaita-siddhi*, p. 576. *jīvasya anavacchinnabrahmānandaprakāśā-nyathānupapattiśca tatra mānam.*

CONCLUSION

The final position of the Advaitin is that *avidyā* is neither positive nor existent. It is an illusory appearance which, from an empirical perspective, seems to exist. But, since it is sublated, its true status is inscrutable. When *Brahman* Which is of the nature of truth, intelligence, and bliss, is seen, the cognition of multiplicity vanishes of its own accord.

Chapter Seven

THE UNTENABILITY OF REMOVABILITY

Introduction

The sixth objection of Rāmānuja, *nivartaka-anupapatti*, contends that *Brahman*-knowledge does not have the capacity to remove or sublate *avidyā*. It is the contention of Advaita that: (1) *avidyā*, though beginningless (*anādi*) has an end. There is no cause to account for *avidyā's* beginning. Things of the world are related as cause and effect. The origination of anything is explained in terms of its cause. However, since *avidyā* is the cause of the entire world, according to Advaita, what can be the cause of *avidyā*? If a beginning were to be ascribed to *avidyā*, then there would have to be a cause for that cause, and so on *ad infinitum*. As well, it is only by presupposing time that one can speak of a beginning for ignorance in time. But time itself is a product of ignorance and so it is a fundamental mistake to even ask such a question. (2) However, *avidyā* has an end. It is not beginningless in a manner identical with *Brahman*, for, if that were the case, there would be no end to it. But ignorance has an end because it vanishes when *Brahman*-knowledge arises. (3) *Avidyā* is not permanent, but is terminated by right knowledge. (4) The nature of this right knowledge which removes *avidyā* is One, non-dual, impartite and undifferentiated.

Rāmānuja's Objection 1

The Viśiṣṭādvaitin contends that there is no knowledge which removes *avidyā*. "It is not true that final release results from the knowledge of a non-differentiated *Brahman*."[1] *Brahman* is not attributeless (*nirguṇa*), and undifferentiated (*nirviśeṣa*). *Brahman* is never found without attributes—"*brahmaṇaḥ saviśeṣatvādeva*"[2]. This is supported by such *śruti* texts as:

1. *Śrī-bhāṣya* I.1.1, p. 73.
2. Ibid.

He Who lives in us as our guide, Who is one, and yet appears in many forms, in Whom the hundred lights of heaven are one, in Whom the *Vedas* are one...[3]

(We adore) the God with a thousand heads, with an all-seeing eye, Who grants peace to all, Nārāyaṇa, Universal God.[4]

As well, the Viśiṣṭādvaitins hold that *janmādyasya yataḥ* is the only definition of *Brahman—Brahman* is the sovereign Lord, the repository of all auspicious qualities like Omniscience, Omnipotence, Bliss, Truth, Mercy, etc. and from Whom proceed the origin, sustenance, and dissolution of this varied and wonderfully fashioned world.[5]

Knowledge requires a knower, an object to be known and the act of knowledge. According to Rāmānuja, not only *Brahman*, but every object of one's knowledge possesses attributes and differentiation. There is no such thing as an attributeless, undifferentiated object of knowledge. That being so, it is an impossibility to obtain knowledge of an attributeless *Brahman*.

Rāmānuja justifies his objection to the claim that *avidyā* may be removed by knowledge of a *nirguṇa Brahman* on the ground that every valid means of knowledge (*pramāṇa*) conveys the knowledge of an object which only possesses attributes (*saviśeṣavastu-viṣayatvāt sarvapramāṇānām*).[6] Neither perception and inference, nor verbal testimony conveys the existence of an object which is attributeless.

Objection Against Perception

It is Rāmānuja's contention that perception gives only *saguṇa*, *saviśeṣa* knowledge. He accepts the classification that perception is of two types: determinate (*savikalpa*) and indeterminate (*nirvikalpa*), though he claims that both types have a content which is only *saviśeṣa*.

Unlike the Advaitins, who contend that *nirvikalpa pratyakṣa* is perception of an attributeless object,[7] Rāmānuja says that it is but

3. *Taittirīya Āraṇyaka* III.13.1; III.11.1.
4. *Mahānārāyaṇa Upaniṣad* I.8.10-11; I.235-36.
5. *Brahma-sūtra* I.1.2.
6. *Śrī-bhāṣya* I.1.1.
7. *Vedānta-paribhāṣā* I, pp. 32-33.

the first stage in the two stages of perception. Indeterminate perception is apprehension of an object for the first time, while determinate perception consists of the subsequent apprehensions of the same object. For example, upon observing a cow for the first time, an individual perceives the animal as qualified by certain attributes, viz., size, shape and so on. This apprehension involves a subject-predicate relation. Any object apprehended for the first time is qualified in a particular way.

The second stage of apprehension involves, not only the apprehension of the object as qualified in a particular way, but also the apprehension of the generic or class level (*jāti*) is added. Thus, after perceiving a cow for the first time, one is able to extend one's knowledge of the special feature of cowness, i.e. a triangular shaped dewlap, which was perceived even in the original perception, and draw the conclusion from this feature that this is a cow.

Advaita's Reply

Advaita agrees with Rāmānuja that determinate perception involves apprehension of an object with attributes. They disagree with each other regarding the perceptual knowledge given in indeterminate perception. Rāmānuja claims that this knowledge is relational, while Advaita claims that it is non-relational. As well, Rāmānuja claims that the difference between determinate and indeterminate perceptual knowledge is one of degree (they are stages in an act of perception), while Advaita claims that there is a qualitative difference between the two. Finally, Rāmānuja claims that indeterminate perceptual knowledge precedes determinate perceptual knowledge, while Advaita reverses this sequence. The expression, 'this is Devadatta' which conveys determinate knowledge, precedes the indeterminate identity judgment, 'this is that Devadatta'.

According to Advaita, the experience of deep sleep disproves Rāmānuja's claim that indeterminate perception is relational. In the state of deep-sleep everyone has the experience of the Self as devoid of all distinctions. When an individual awakes and recalls his or her deep-sleep experience, the individual says that he or she was not aware of anything during that experience. There was neither an objective bodily awareness nor a subjective conscious self-awareness. However, merely because the mind and the senses were not conveying information during deep-sleep, it does not mean that Consciousness was not present.

The Advaitin accepts that there is both an intentional consciousness, facilitated by the mind and senses, and a Consciousness qua Consciousness which is not a 'consciousness-of' but a 'Consciousness-as-it-is'. Any recollection presupposes the prior experience of what is recollected. In this example, the Self or bare Consciousness devoid of any distinctions is what is experienced in deep-sleep and recalled by the waking 'I'.

During deep-sleep, the knower, the known and the act of knowledge (*tripuṭī*) are all absent. As mentioned earlier, the Advaitin recognizes existence of the witness self (*sākṣin*) and *avidyā-vṛtti* during the state of deep-sleep. But there is no relational knowledge at that time due to the absence of the *tripuṭī*. Advaita maintains that the deep-sleep experience, nonetheless, demonstrates that indeterminate knowledge is relationless because, upon waking, the sleeping individual says, 'I slept happily seeing nothing, observing nothing, not even myself'. And this experience validates and resonates with the *śruti* text which says, 'The Self is one only without a second.'[8]

Reply 2

Advaita agreed with Rāmānuja that *savikalpa* perception gives relational knowledge. However they disagreed over *nirvikalpa* perception—does it give the knowledge of pure Being or does it give generic and other features which distinguish the object from other objects?

Advaita maintains that every object, in every cognition, is cognized as existent. They go further and maintain that it is only *sat* or existence which is correctly cognized and that the distinguishing features such as name and form which are perceived are erroneous.

Next, the Advaitin says that the *sat* or existent which is cognized in all perceptions is *Brahman*. The real is the existent and the existent alone is the real. Thus, the world of name and form is not real, and consequently not actually existent. It is said to be existent by courtesy only, from an empirical point of view.

8. *Chāndogya Upaniṣad* VI.2.1.

If this is true, then what is the explanation for the world being cognized—even at the empirical level? The Advaitin maintains that this existence which is ascribed to the world is due to a false identification of the world with *Brahman*. The world appears to exist because of the substratum, *Brahman*, upon Which it is superimposed.

The consequences of this mean, that in every perception, what is perceived as existent is *Brahman* alone and it is the existence of *Brahman* which is apprehended in every act of perception. The cognition of the world is but a false superimposition upon that which is. When an individual says, 'this is a rock', the word 'this' refers to what is existent, i.e. *Brahman*, and the words 'is a rock' refer to a false superimposition thereon.

The 'this' which is perceived in any perception is never sublated, while the 'rock' suffers sublation. Generally it is held that the attributes which objects possess are real, along with the object itself. So how can one claim that the evidence which perception gives is false? The Advaitin claims that what is sublated is unreal. Everything other than *Brahman* suffers sublation. Thus, *Brahman* alone is real.

Reply 3

Rāmānuja's position is that difference is apprehended by perception. According to him, the distinctive form (*saṃsthāna*) of an object, as well as its generic quality (*jāti*), is revealed in *savikalpa* perception. This generic form is distinctive and different (*bheda*) and to perceive an object is to perceive its distinctive form; to perceive its distinctive form is to perceive its *jāti*; and to perceive its *jāti* is to perceive its difference.[9]

Now, *saṃsthāna* means a distinctive form of an object.[10] Rāmānuja argues that an object's generic quality is the same as an object's distinctiveness.[11] Then he goes on to say the same with regard to equating *jāti* and *bheda*. An individual can distinguish one object from another, e.g., a cow from a horse, merely by apprehending its *jāti*. To quote Rāmānuja, Perception is the ap-

9. *Śrī-bhāṣya* I.1.1.
10. Ibid.
11. Ibid.

prehension of an object associated with *bheda* which is of the nature of *jāti*, which again is only *saṃsthāna—vastusaṃsthānarūpa-jātyādilakṣaṇa-bheda-viśiṣṭaviṣayameva pratyakṣam.*[12]

Advaita regards this position of Rāmānuja as untenable. In the first place, *saṃsthāna* is not the same as *jāti*. One and the same 'dewlap' (*saṃsthāna*) is not present in every cow—though every cow possesses the generic feature (*jāti*) of 'cowness'. Nor is the generic feature (*jāti*) the same as difference (*bheda*). To say that a given object is different from another object is not the same as to say that a given object has the same generic quality of another object.

The fact is, that both distinctiveness and generic feature are indicators of difference. The former brings out the difference between two objects of the same class. The latter brings out the difference between two objects belonging to different classes.

As well, the knowledge of difference presupposes the knowledge of the correlate, while neither distinctiveness nor generic features require this knowledge of the correlate. To say, 'The rock is different' remains inconclusive until one knows what it is different from, but neither distinctiveness nor generic features contain this expectation.

Objection Against Inference

Rāmānuja claims that inference can also demonstrate that all knowledge is *saviśeṣa*. Inference is based upon perception. An inference has to fulfil two conditions in order to be valid: (1) the middle term (*hetu*) must be observed as being present in the minor term (*pakṣa*); (2) there must be a knowledge of the invariable concomitance (*vyāpti*) between the middle and major (*sādhya*) terms.

Neither condition, by itself, can lead to a valid inferential conclusion. It is a combination of the two which is necessary to serve as the instrument of inference. Since the first condition demands a perception of the minor term as characterized by the middle term, this reveals that inference is dependent upon perception. Rāmānuja, therefore, concludes that if an object is known through perception to be *saviśeṣa*, then it follows that all inferences must be *saviśeṣa* also.[13]

12. Ibid.
13. *Śrī-bhāṣya* I.1.1.

REPLY

Advaita contends that inference can also show that *Brahman* is *nirviśeṣa*. Rāmānuja's claim is incorrect that perception, and thus inference, points towards all objects as being *saviśeṣa*. It is a well-known dictum that the particular points to the universal. Thus, the following inference: (1) This world has for its source *Brahman* Which is general. (2) Because it is a particular. (3) Whatever is a particular arises from the general.

Or, there is the following argument: (1) *Brahman*/*Ātman* is *nirviśeṣa*. (2) Because It is experienced without qualities in deep-sleep. (3) Whatever is experienced without qualities is *nirviśeṣa*.

VERBAL TESTIMONY

Verbal testimony is of two kinds: empirical (*laukika*) and Scriptural (*vaidika*). Scriptural testimony conveys the knowledge, not of a *nirguṇa Brahman*, but of a *saguṇa Brahman*, according to Rāmānuja. He says:

> Scriptural texts like, 'I have known the great Being *resplendent like the sun* and Who is beyond this darkness of ignorance; knowing Him alone one attains immortality here—there is no other way to go by', (*Śvet*. III.18) show that *Brahman* is differentiated and that the knowledge of such a *Brahman* alone leads to liberation.[14]

Rāmānuja's arguments take two forms—the first one a general argument concerning empirical verbal testimony and the nature of a sentence, and the second argument, a specific one in the form of a detailed examination of some scriptural texts.

ARGUMENT 1

Verbal testimony is comprised of, and functions through, a set of words or sentences. To obtain the meaning of a sentence, one must relate one word to another. And each word is comprised of a root/base (*prakṛti*) plus a suffix (*pratyaya*). This demonstrates that each word is a complex phenomenon comprised of two or more parts. It, therefore, follows that a sentence is a complex whole as well. Since the meanings conveyed by the stem and the suffix

14. Ibid., p. 73.

are different, individual words and composite sentences must needs convey a relational meaning. Thus, Rāmānuja concludes that neither an individual word, nor a sentence is capable of denoting an object which is *nirviśeṣa*.[15]

REPLY

According to Advaita, the meaning of a word or sentence can only be determined by taking into consideration the intention (*tātparya*) of the speaker.[16] What a word or a sentence purports to convey is, indeed, its meaning. This is cryptically stated as: *yatparaś śabdaḥ sa śabdārthaḥ*. Sometimes a word or sentence purports to convey a relational meaning and sometimes it conveys a non-relational one.

A sentence such as, 'this rock is heavy', conveys a relational meaning. But a sentence like, 'this is that Devadatta' conveys a non-relational sense. This latter sentence conveys a sense of identity because that is its purport. It means that Devadatta who is seen in *this* place, at *this* time, is identical with *that* Devadatta who was seen in *that* place, at *that* time. The identity is in respect of the person concerned and not with regard to the place and time. The time and place both differ, as does Devadatta's body itself. Formerly he was thin and now he is fat. Still, the bare substantive, Devadatta, is one and the same minus all of his incompatible determinants.

ARGUMENT 2

Rāmānuja contends that all *śruti* texts teach that *Brahman* is *saguṇa* and *saviśeṣa*. For instance, Rāmānuja interprets the text, "*Brahman* is real (*satyam*), knowledge (*jñānam*), and infinite (*anantam*)", as demonstrating that *Brahman* is qualified by the attributes: *satyam, jñānam* and *anantam*.

According to the grammatical rule of co-ordination (*sāmānādhikaraṇya*), there is a grammatical co-ordinate relation between the three words, '*satyam, jñānam* and *anantam*'. Whenever such a relation exists, whatever the words denote is a given thing as qualified by several attributes. In this example the three words are not

15. *Śrī-bhāṣya* I.1.1.
16. *Vedānta-paribhāṣā* IV, p. 106.

synonyms. Thus, it is logical to conclude, says Rāmānuja, that these three words qualify *Brahman* by qualities which inhere in It.

There is one big advantage to Rāmānuja's interpretation and that is by interpreting these three words as attributes, the text can be read in its primary sense (*mukhyārtha*). There is a general rule of interpretation that says that whenever the primary meaning holds good, one should not resort to a secondary meaning.

REPLY

According to Advaita, this text conveys a non-relational meaning. Normally a sentence is held to convey a relation of duality and the meaning of the sentence is conveyed through the relation obtained among the various words comprising it which convey difference. The contention is that a relational sentence cannot give a non-relational meaning. Generally, when two or more words are in grammatical co-ordination, the thing referred to is not different though the meanings of the two or more words are, i.e. blue lotus. When the connotations are different, one usually imagines that the denotations are also different. For instance, 'blue lotus' designates a subject-predicate relation of the qualified (lotus) and its attribute (blueness). Though the two words have different individual meanings, since they are in grammatical co-ordination, the thing referred to is one, i.e. lotus. Thus the sentence connotes a single object with attributes. The example of 'blue lotus' refers to a oneness with relation, but there are also statements which reveal perfect identity (according to Advaita). In fact, it is just overcoming any idea of difference which is the purpose of an identity statement.

Literally it would seem that the words which comprise an identity statement (*akhaṇḍārtha-vākya*) are not synonymous and thus one must resort to some sort of secondary meaning if one wishes to make such statements meaningful. 'This is that Devadatta' or '*satyam, jñānam, anantam*' seems to reveal a *prima facie* absurdity.

The issue is to explain how a verbal sense can give a non-verbal meaning or how a relational sense can give a non-relational meaning. If it can, is this meaning a primary or secondary one? When there is a relation of duality, the meaning of a sentence is conveyed through the relation obtained among the words conveying difference. Sentences which convey a relation of non-duality, however, give an impartite sense. Though the words are non-synonymous, yet they have the same referent. This shows that it is possible for a relational sentence to convey a non-relational meaning. For instance, in answering the question, 'which is the sun?', it is the identity of the object that is being conveyed and not the relation of luminosity to the sun. In answering the question, 'what is *Brahman*?', it is the identity of *Brahman* as *satyam, jñānam, anantam,* that is being conveyed.

Satyam, jñānam, anantam expresses knowledge of a single object (*Brahman*) by definition or description. Usually a description expresses a relation of one thing to another. But in impartite statements, the individual words of the sentence refer only to one entity. Whether it be, 'the present President of the United States is Reagan' or '*satyam, jñānam, anantam*', both expressions convey only identity.

Usually *satyam, jñānam, anantam* is interpreted in a secondary sense because *Brahman* is considered to be beyond all determinations and attributes. Thus *satyam* is used to indicate that *Brahman* is not unreal; *jñānam* is used to indicate that *Brahman* is not what is unconscious; and *anantam* is used to indicate that *Brahman* is not finite.[17]

According to Vimuktātman, *Brahman* is *satyam, jñānam* and *anantam.* The terms are not synonymous so there is no repetition. Yet, being non-synonymous, the terms do not indicate diverse attributes either. *Brahman* is one and non-dual and to interpret such statements in a secondary meaning is merely a philosophical ploy to get over the charge of repetition if the terms are said to be synonymous. And if the terms are said to be non-synonymous, then these terms become diverse attributes which belie the Advaitin's doctrine of non-duality. Yet, according to Vimuktātman, such a ploy is not necessary.

Advaita overcomes the difficulty of multiplicity by dissolving the apparent reality of the empirical world. It declares that multiplicity is illusory from the standpoint of *Brahman* as-it-is and what is left is *Brahman* alone.

17. Among others Vimuktātman in his *Iṣṭa-siddhi* pp. 26-32 shows how this expression can be interpreted in a literal or primary sense.

OBJECTION 2

According to Rāmānuja, the oneness or non-duality of *Brahman* is not a bare oneness devoid of distinctions. In addition to its infiniteness of auspicious qualities, *Brahman* is also conceived of as an integral unity. This unity unifies the empirical multiplicity of qualities without depriving them of their individuality or denying itself of transcendence.

Regarding the text, "(*Brahman* is) the witness, the knower, the only one, devoid of qualities",[18] the words 'devoid of qualities' (*nirguṇa*) do not convey the idea that *Brahman* is devoid of qualities. Rāmānuja contends that *Brahman* is *nirguṇa* only in the sense that It has no evil qualities associated with *prakṛti*.[19] It is the contention of the Viśiṣṭādvaitins that there is a distinction between sacred qualities and profane qualities and that expressions such as *nirguṇa* point to this distinction.

REPLY 2

According to Advaita, Rāmānuja commits a double mistake in his interpretation of the word '*nirguṇa*' in the above text. This word occurs in the text without any qualification, and, in the absence of any qualifying terms, there is no justification for saying that the term '*nirguṇa*' means 'without evil qualities associated with *prakṛti*'. Not only does Rāmānuja ignore the obvious meaning of the term, but he also suggests another meaning which is not warranted.

OBJECTION 3

Rāmānuja interprets the Upaniṣadic 'Great Saying' (*mahāvākya*) in a manner at odds with the Advaita interpretation. According to Rāmānuja, in the saying, That thou art, *tat tvam asi,* the word *tvam,* which commonly stands for the individual soul, in this case really points to God Who is the individual soul's inner self (*antaryāmin*). What the term *tat* refers to is this same God, but viewed from the perspective of the cause of the universe. The identity meant by the expression, *tat tvam asi,* therefore, points to the fact that God, as the indweller of the individual soul and God

18. *Śvetāśvatara Upaniṣad* VI.11.
19. *Śrī-bhāṣya* I.1.1, pp. 77-78.

as the source of the universe, though real and distinct, are one in their inseparable relationship in God.[20]

Reply 3

According to Advaita, the primary meaning of the saying, *tat tvam asi,* is seemingly absurd. The term '*tvam*' signifies an individual soul, complete with its limiting adjuncts of the mind-body complex, finiteness, mortality, etc. The term '*tat*' signifies *Brahman,* complete with its adjuncts of remoteness, omniscience, omnipotence, etc. How can the limited individual soul be identical with the unlimited Supreme Being? How can humanity and Divinity be one and the same?

Evidently the two terms, '*tat*' and '*tvam*', in their primary meaning, do not refer to one and the same entity. Thus, there is an apparent contradiction in the *mahāvākya.* However, if the primary meanings of a sentence prove to be inadequate for an intelligible understanding, then their implied or secondary meanings must be sought.

According to Advaita, both terms, '*tat*' and '*tvam*' refer to the same unqualified Pure Consciousness, the Ground of both, *Brahman* Itself. This understanding is accomplished by cancelling the adjuncts of both terms and letting the non-verbal import of the expression reveal itself.

There are three steps in this process. In step one, the words of the *mahāvākya* are noted to be in grammatical co-ordination. Generally speaking, when there is grammatical co-ordination between two terms, their connotations are different but their denotations are the same, e.g., 'a blue lotus' connotes two things, blueness and lotusness, but it denotes only one entity, a lotus.

In step two, a subject-predicate relation (*viśeṣaṇa-viśeṣya-jñāna*) is noted as being present. These are of two types: a relation of duality (*bheda-saṃsarga*), i.e. blue lotus; and a relation of non-duality (*abheda-saṃsarga*), i.e. *tat tvam asi.* A subject-predicate relation is one between the qualifier and the qualified and, though such a relation obtains between blue and lotus, it will not work with *tat* and *tvam. Tvam* cannot be an attribute of *tat.*

In step three, an indirect meaning is applied (*lakṣya-lakṣaṇa-*

20. Ibid., pp. 73-76.

sambandha-jñāna). One gives up the primary meaning of *tat* and *tvam*. Their adjuncts are given up since they are opposed in meaning and one is left with Pure Consciousness. The same Consciousness which is the essence of both *Brahman* and the *jīva* is identical once the limiting adjuncts have been removed.[21]

ARGUMENT 3

Rāmānuja contends that *Brahman* is *saguṇa* so how can one obtain knowledge of a non-existent entity—a *nirguṇa Brahman*? If this knowledge cannot be obtained, and it cannot be according to Rāmānuja, then how can *avidyā* be removed by a non-dual knowledge which does not exist?

According to Advaita, *avidyā* is said to be inexplicable or *anirvacanīya*. As well, this ignorance is said to be removed by knowledge. Rāmānuja draws the conclusion that if *avidyā* is *anirvacanīya*, and its antidote is knowledge, then this said knowledge must be definable or *nirvacanīya*.

However, if knowledge is definable, the question is asked: Is it real, unreal, both real and unreal, or something else altogether?

Obviously this knowledge cannot be something else altogether, simply because no one can conceive of what that would be. It cannot be unreal because, even according to you, the unreal is totally non-existent. Nor can it be both, for that violates the law of non-contradiction.

Thus, the Advaitin's knowledge must be real. If this is so, is it real as: identical with *Brahman* (*svarūpa-jñāna*) or different (*vṛtti-jñāna*)? It cannot be identical with *Brahman* because even the Advaitin says that *Brahman* is not opposed to ignorance. And if it is identical with *Brahman* and thus not opposed to ignorance, how is it that you say that it is opposed to ignorance? Or, if it is real and identical with *Brahman,* then because *Brahman* is ever-existent, there could not be ignorance at all. And if it is different from *Brahman,* and real, then dualism occurs.

Rāmānuja's position is that *avidyā* is identical with *karma*. *Avidyā* is real and cannot be removed by knowledge alone. Knowledge is one of the aids to its removal, but ultimately ignorance is removed by the Grace of God—which is won by disinterested action (*niṣkāma-karma*). The text says:

21. *Naiṣkarmya-siddhi,* Chapter 3.

> This self cannot be attained by any amount of teaching or great intellect. It cannot be known even through a wide learning. The self reveals itself to him, whom God chooses.[22]

There is also an alternative to God's Grace, according to Viśiṣṭādvaita. Liberation can be won through devotion (*bhakti*). *Karma-yoga* and *jñāna-yoga* help produce *bhakti-yoga*. The former consists in doing one's duties without attaching any importance to the fruits which may result from it. The latter prepares the way for concentrating one's own self as detached from the bondage of ignorance and as essentially subservient to the will of God.

22. *Kaṭha Upaniṣad* I.2.23.

CHAPTER EIGHT

IGNORANCE IS NOT REMOVED BY BRAHMAN KNOWLEDGE

INTRODUCTION

Rāmānuja's final major objection, *nivṛtti-anupapatti,* against the Advaitin's doctrine of *avidyā* contends that ignorance cannot be removed at all. He argues that since bondage is real, the knowledge of the identity of *Brahman* and the *Ātman* cannot remove it. It is only by the Grace of God that ignorance can be removed. He says;

> Bondage is real and is the result of ignorance which is of the nature of *karma* without a beginning. This bondage can be destroyed only through Knowledge, i.e. through the Knowledge that *Brahman* is the inner ruler different from souls and matter. Such knowledge alone leads to final release or *mokṣa.* This Knowledge is attained through the Grace of the Lord pleased by the due performance of the daily duties prescribed for different castes and stages of life, duties performed not with the idea of attaining any results but with the idea of propitiating the Lord.[1]

This much we observed in the previous chapter. The question that now arises is: If bondage is real, how can it be removed by knowledge of *Brahman*? Whatever is real cannot be sublated. The function of knowledge is to reveal a thing, not to destroy it. For example, knowledge of a rock reveals that rock, it does not destroy it. Knowledge is declared to be controlled by the already existent reality.[2] Thus, knowledge is revelatory and merely gives information. Advaita claims, in response, that the cause of bondage is ignorance and ignorance can only be removed by knowledge. This we have observed earlier.

1. *Śrī-bhāṣya* I.1.1, p. 80.
2. *Brahma sūtra-bhāṣya* I.1.2. *vastu-yāthātmyajñānam.*

Objection 1

The Viśiṣṭādvaitin asks, 'How do you say that bondage is illusory (*mithyā*)?' There is no evidence or *pramāṇa* for such a claim. According to us, the individual experiences, pleasure and pain, which are caused by *karma* through many births and deaths. (According to Advaita, these are caused by *avidyā*). If one were to follow the Advaitin's advice, instead of removing bondage, it would only be strengthened. How is that? Because *Brahman* is *saguṇa* and so to seek for a knowledge of a *nirguṇa Brahman* would not only be false, but also futile. For, in reality, there is no such thing. Knowledge of a thing must accord with the thing and since all objects are *saguṇa*, there is no such thing as *nirguṇa* knowledge.

Objection 2

What is the ontological status of this knowledge which you say removes ignorance? Is it real or unreal? According to Advaita, it must be unreal or else dualism will result. Thus, if it is unreal, do you call it *mithyā*? This is an absurd position because Advaita calls knowledge *mithyā* and *avidyā mithyā*. Such a situation cannot be. And if knowledge is *mithyā*, what will remove it? Another unreal knowledge? This will lead to a *regressus ad infinitum*.

Reply

Advaita says that this saving knowledge is momentary. Once it has accomplished its work, it too vanishes of its own accord. Thus, it does not require anything else to remove it. This needs some explanation.

Is the eradication of ignorance real or unreal? If it is real, then is it as real as *Brahman*? This would produce a dualism. If it is unreal, then there is no removal of ignorance at all. The same consequences apply if the eradication of ignorance is said to be inexplicable. Yet, when all is said and done, the fact of the cessation of ignorance is well-known and cannot be disputed.

The objection is: If the removal of ignorance is real, then there will be a second reality. If it is *Brahman* Itself, then *Brahman* being eternal, the absence of ignorance will also be eternal, in which case there will be no ignorance to account for the cause of the world. And ignorance, too, will be causeless. If ignorance has a cause, then *Brahman* too, being identical with ignorance, will have a cause and cease thereby to be *Brahman*. Nor will there be a locus for ignorance, since *Brahman* will be non-eternal.

If the removal of ignorance is non-existence, then if the non-existence, too, is *Brahman,* then all the difficulties of the non-existence of *Brahman* will arise. If this removal is an attribute of *Brahman,* then this attribute is either different or non-different from *Brahman*. If it is either, the above difficulties will arise.

If the removal of ignorance is unreal, the world will become real. It cannot be both real and unreal. If it is indeterminable, the same ignorance which is also indeterminable will exist and there will be no liberation. It cannot be void (*śūnya*) for the void is not the ultimate goal of life, nor can it be established.

Now, the Advaitin says that in addition to the four forms of removal given, e.g., real, unreal, real and unreal, and indeterminable, there is a fifth alternative. These four forms pertain only to determinable entities. But the removal of ignorance must be of another nature. For ignorance is not a determinable entity.

The destruction of ignorance does not originate anything else. If it could, the only possibility would be *Brahman*—but this is untenable because *Brahman* is unoriginated. Yet, surely ignorance is destroyed, though this destruction is not established by any *pramāṇa*. *Pramāṇas* dispel ignorance and render things known. But if the removal of ignorance was established by a *pramāṇa*, this would entail the prior establishment of its ignorance, and so on *ad infinitum*.

Ignorance is inert as are its products, the objects of experience. Thus, the destruction of an inert ignorance must be accomplished by something sentient. In other words, ignorance cannot be its own destroyer. It is well-known that knowledge removes ignorance. However, even this knowledge is not real—for we know that *Brahman* is the locus of ignorance. Thus the destruction of ignorance must not be ontologically real. The destruction of the unreal can never render it real. Remember, knowledge cannot create anything, it merely reveals.

Just as fire accompanied by the wind consumes dry grass, so does *Brahman,* with the help of knowledge, consume ignorance. And in the process, the knowledge itself also gets consumed. Once the fuel has been exhausted, both the grass and the fire are destroyed. The other popular example to illustrate this phenomenon is the use of a thorn to remove a thorn or splinter in one's finger. Once the thorn in one's finger has been removed by the second thorn, both thorns are no longer needed and are thrown away.

How can an unreal ignorance be removed by an unreal knowledge? Though *śruti*, and therefore the *vṛtti-jñāna* given by it, is unreal, still it is accepted as a valid means of knowledge. There is no contradiction here. Anything that is produced is not real. Even the cognition which has *Brahman* for its content is produced by *śruti*, and is thus not real. There is nothing strange here, for the Advaitin is merely saying that a non-real *śruti* is the cause of a non-real cognition. And this non-real cognition removes ignorance, which is also non-real, and then both of them disappear together.

Objection 3

Vedānta Deśika objects to the contention that *avidyā* is removed by non-dual knowledge. He asks, 'What is the nature of this knowledge?' Is it: (1) different from the knowledge which constitutes the essential nature of *Brahman*? (2) non-different from it? (3) both different and non-different? (4) neither different nor non-different? (5) something else?[3]

Regarding the first alternative, does the knowledge in question have any content or not? If it is without content, it ceases to be knowledge. If it has a content, then what is this content? Is it *Brahman,* or is it knowledge associated with ignorance or something else or illusoriness of everything other than *Brahman*?

If *Brahman* is the content of the sublating knowledge, it would be identical with the essence of *Brahman* and as such, could not remove ignorance. For such a knowledge to be able to remove ignorance, *Brahman*-knowledge itself would have to be destroyed.

If the Advaitin argues that he makes a distinction between two kinds of knowledge, this still will not help. *Brahman*-knowledge is of the nature of the substrate which is the locus for ignorance. Hence, it cannot remove ignorance. And to say that it is the knowledge of a mental mode does not help either, because since this knowledge is unreal, it cannot remove ignorance being of the nature of illusion itself.

If it is said that *Brahman* as associated with ignorance is the

3. *Śatadūṣaṇī*, *Vāda* 43.

content of the sublating knowledge, that too, is untenable. If the mental mode has for its content *Brahman* associated with ignorance, then like the witness-consciousness, it would not remove ignorance. The witness-consciousness does not remove illusion, but on the contrary, it is favourable to illusion in so far as it manifests it.

Nor can it be the third alternative that something other than *Brahman* is the content of the sublating knowledge. For, in that case, there is absolutely no chance of its being the sublater since, that itself is of the nature of illusion.

Nor can it be maintained that the manifestation of things outside *Brahman* as illusory is the content of the final mental mode. For, without knowing the substrate of illusion, it is not possible to know the illusory character of things. As well, if this mental mode which is supposed to remove ignorance apprehends its content, i.e. illusoriness of everything except *Brahman,* and accepts it as real, then duality appears. If it is apprehended as unreal, then it would follow that the world illusion is real.

The third, fourth, and fifth alternatives are also untenable as they are self-contradictory. Nor could this knowledge be said to be non-different from *Brahman.* If *Brahman*-knowledge were said to remove ignorance, then there would be no ignorance at all—since *Brahman* is eternal and beginningless. Nor can *Brahman* be said to be the cause of the world-appearance, as well as its destruction, because this would be self-contradictory.

According to Vedānta Deśika, the very conception of the destruction or removal of ignorance is unintelligible. Advaita claims that with the onset of *Brahman*-knowledge, *avidyā* disappears. But Vedānta Deśika asks whether this disappearance of ignorance is real or unreal. If it is illusory, then there is not a complete destruction of ignorance. As well, if ignorance is said to be destroyed, and it has its locus in *Brahman*, then *Brahman*, too, must undergo change—which is contrary to Scripture.

It may be said that the function of the destruction of ignorance is to show that everything other than *Brahman* is illusory. As soon as this function has accomplished its work, it, too, is destroyed. But this is untenable. If the destruction of *avidyā* itself ceases to exist, and is illusory itself, then that would mean that there is a destruction of the destruction which means either that ignorance is again restored or that it is real.

All of these arguments go to show that *avidyā* cannot be destroyed. The crux of the issue is: If *avidyā* is different from *Brahman*, then Advaita breaks down. And if *avidyā* is not different from *Brahman*, then *Brahman* can never free Itself of ignorance.

Reply

Advaita says that *avidyā* is a unique phenomenon, something *sui generis*. It is not real enough to set itself up as a rival to *Brahman*, and yet it is not unreal or non-existent like the son of a barren woman. The bottom line is that while *avidyā* is an empirical fact, *Brahman* is an eternal Reality. Individuals on the street consider ignorance as real. Knowers of *Brahman* consider it as unreal. Those who enquire into it, consider it neither real nor unreal, but inexplicable. It is the failure of Advaita's critics to note the relative status of *avidyā* which prompts their criticisms. Sometimes the critics take *avidyā* to be nothing more than a psychological state and a lack of knowledge. But, in actuality, psychological ignorance is only a function of *avidyā* itself. It is part of its power of obscuration. It is true that *avidyā* has a universal reference and status—however, and this is crucial, its status is relative or empirical and its context must always be kept in mind.

CHAPTER NINE

CONCLUSION

The polemics between the Advaitins and the Viśiṣṭādvaitins seems unending. It has continued for over seven hundred years and shows no signs of abating. Though both sides are but a systematic exposition of an accepted canonical literature, they disagree over virtually everything—ranging from a theory of knowledge all the way to eschatological, cosmological and ontological considerations.

After the initial formulation of the Advaita philosophy by Śaṅkara, both schools have grown out of critical reflections on and from previous philosophical positions. They both have roots which go back into the mists of history and each exegesis claims to be a faithful explication of the 'true' meaning of the *śruti*. For, after all, both philosophical systems are but deductive interpretations. They both assumed the validity of Bādarāyaṇa's *sūtras* and then 'unfolded' its meaning as implied by the relevant Upaniṣadic statements.[1]

Both systems assert that the *Vedas* are *apauruṣeya*, and hence unquestionable. However, they both also assert that the principal primary means of liberation is *jñāna* according to Advaita and *bhakti* according to Viśiṣṭādvaita. In order to make this intelligible, they have to emphasise certain scriptural passages instead of others, and interpret them to suit their own standpoint.

It is this fact, that the Upaniṣadic statements can be interpreted

1. The *raison d'etre* for the *Brahma-sūtra* is to prove the rightness of the Upaniṣadic texts as having one particular meaning and no other, by means of scriptural texts (*śruti*), reasoning (*yukti*), and experience (*anubhava*). The *Brahma-sūtra* itself, contains 4 chapters (*adhyāya*) and each chapter has 4 parts (*pāda*). The parts are divided into subject-matters (*adhikaraṇa*). Each *adhikaraṇa* contains a sentence (*viṣaya-vākya*) from the *Upaniṣads*. For example, first *sūtra*, '*athāto brahma-jijñāsā*', contains the thesis (*viṣaya*) 'you should desire to know *Brahman*' from the *Bṛhadāraṇyaka Upaniṣad* wherein Yājñavalkya is speaking to Maitreyī. The *viṣaya-vākya* is 'the Self ought to be known'. The *adhikaraṇa* is '*jijñāsā-adhikaraṇa*'.

differently, which accounts for the differences among the Vedāntic systems. However, there are certain common premises which are shared by the two systems: (1) Both accept that 'an enquiry into the nature of *Brahman*' is the sole purpose of all the Vedāntic systems.[2] (Though they differ over the prerequisites involved.) (2) Both accept that the world has a cause.[3] (Though they differ over its ontological status.) (3) Both accept that 'the real is eternal'. (Though Advaita takes this definition literally while Viśiṣṭādvaita qualifies it.) (4) Both accept the self-evident existence of the soul. (Though they differ over the status of its consciousness.) (5) Both accept the concepts of 'ignorance' and 'bondage'. (Though they differ over their reality.) (6) They both accept the concept of liberation. (Though Advaita calls it non-dual and Viśiṣṭādvaita maintains that it is with distinctions.)

Exponents of Indian thought have given a lot of weight to the two concepts of action (*karma*) and spiritual practices (*sādhana*). In this regard, it is a common theme to speak of the 'qualified spiritual aspirant' or *adhikārī*. Due to an individual's predilections, qualifications, capacities and achievements, there are said to be individual differences between *adhikārins*. Thus, the idea developed that an individual's spiritual training should be suited to the climate of one's mind and heart. Incidentally, this also plays a major role in the continuing existence and proliferation of the Indian pantheon.

In this regard, Advaita Vedānta is often given the pride of place as a philosophical system because it provides the means for accommodating the other Vedāntic attitudes and practices—while the later schools do not, and cannot, admit many of Advaita's theories. And apart from a determination by dialectics, Advaita also enjoys the proof of the Advaitic *anubhava* or experience. The historical examples, even in modern times, ranging from Śrī-Rāmakrishna to Ramana Maharshi, have shown by their utterances and activities that the lofty heights of Advaita need have no quarrel with the other Vedāntic systems' emphasis on consecrated *karma* and confluent devotion. Even if the other systems cannot accommodate Advaita within their schemes of thought and

2. *Brahma-sūtra* I.1.1, *athāto brahma-jijñāsā*.
3. Ibid., I.1.2, *janmādyasya yataḥ*.

activity, Advaita has room for a synthesis and all-encompassing harmony.

As a philosophical system, Advaita embodies the characteristic genius of India's cultural and spiritual legacy—a legacy which is 'unity in diversity'. Within its vast portals, it includes all other variations of thought, in some form or other, at some level or other. It embodies a fellowship in the spiritual quest which is sustained by a fidelity to a common source.

In order to get a correct understanding of Advaitic thought, it is crucial that its fundamental concepts are understood properly. The first and foremost of these concepts is *avidyā/māyā*. Multiplicity exists in and through a conscious experience of it. Advaita explains this seeming experience of the duality of the physical universe by means of the concept of *avidyā/māyā*. This concept is presupposed in their explanation of: the appearance of the world; the one Reality appearing as God and individuals; the distinction between attributeless *Brahman* and a *Brahman* with attributes; in the subject-object dichotomy; the problem of truth and error; the problem of bondage and liberation and the discipline leading thereto. Everywhere one turns, this doctrine of *avidyā/māyā* rears its head. Proclaiming that in truth there is only one indivisible Reality, Advaita attempts to explain the individual's experience of duality by this concept.

We noted that this concept is so important to Advaita that its critics have gone to the extent of labelling Advaita as *māyā-vāda*. Viśiṣṭādvaita realized that Advaita, and therefore this concept, was the major obstacle to establishing its own system. Thus, instead of waiting for the second chapter of the *Brahma-sūtra* (which is known as *avirodhādhyāya*—removal of the opponents' views—wherein one proceeds to meet the objections brought against the views which are set forth in the first chapter and criticises them, showing that a criticism of the rival school's views is essential for building one's own system of philosophy) Rāmānuja launches an all-out major set of objections (*sapta-vidhā anupapatti*) in the opening section of the book itself.

In the course of this book an attempt has been made to give an exposition of the concept of *avidyā/māyā* as set forth by Advaita Vedānta. It has included the major objections against this doctrine as set forth by Rāmānuja and Vedānta Deśika, along with possible rejoinders to these criticisms.

The aim of this book has been to explicate the doctrine of *avidyā/māyā* as established by Advaita, both by exposition as well as rejoinder to stated objections thereto. It has raised several issues which have epistemological, metaphysical, and eschatological ramifications. Though the dialectics meanders here and there, the central theme concerns *Brahman*. After all, Advaita is *Brahma-vāda* and not *māyā-vāda*. This is the main thesis of Advaita and everything else emerges out of it. The central question concerns whether this *Brahman* is *nirguṇa* or *saguṇa*.

The doctrine of *avidyā* has been examined from seven major angles: (1) What is the locus of *avidyā*? (2) Can *avidyā* obscure the nature of *Brahman*? (3) What is the nature of *avidyā*? (4) *Avidyā's* description as inexplicable is untenable; (5) No *pramāṇa* supports a theory of *avidyā*; (6) Can *avidyā* be removed by right knowledge? and (7) The very conception of the cessation of *avidyā* is absurd.

Advaita's doctrine of *avidyā* has been criticised from the angle of: (1) valid means of knowledge (*pramāṇa*), (2) another school's own philosophical position (*siddhānta*), and (3) an acceptance for argument's sake of Advaita's position and then demonstrating that it is still rife with inconsistencies. The first angle of criticism gains its greatest force from that aspect of it which is based on logic or reasoning. The two *pramāṇas*, perception and verbal testimony, though powerful, are limited in a philosophical debate since preconceptions and definitions differ. But inference partakes of the same canons of logic and therefore applies across the board. The validity of the second angle of criticism depends almost entirely on the soundness of the theory which is being presented by the critic himself. And the last angle of criticism is considered by many to be the soundest, from a purely philosophical point of view, since it arises from a lack of internal coherences which are anathema to any particular philosophical system's credibility.

The value of polemic works is that they invariably end in construction. The Indian philosophical systems have employed polemics both as a necessary and desirable part of their history. Their main function was not so much to refute a particular system, though that certainly played a part, as to define and distinguish their own position vis-a-vis that of the other systems. The main purpose of such works is to become clearer on the doctrine itself, as well as to clarify one's position for others. The goal is clarity rather than demolition. What is implicit becomes explicit through such an endeavour. This is the great value of a polemic work.

Though this work places a greater emphasis on the viewpoint as advocated by Advaita Vedānta, it notes that all the Vedāntic systems trace their lineage to the *Vedas*. By exemplifying the Indian dictum, 'unity in diversity', there appears to be a time, place and purpose for each system. There seems to be a historic need for each school of thought. With the great diversity of human predilections, action, devotion and knowledge, everything seems to have its reason to be. India, more than any other nation, seems to have understood this everyday fact of experience. The conflicts which exist between the various systems of philosophy do not seem to affect their value as a particular system of thought. One may even go so far as to claim that the various systems enrich and inspire each other with their mutual fecundity.

BIBLIOGRAPHY

Primary Sources

Advaita-siddhi of Madhusūdana Sarasvatī (Nirnayasagar Press, Bombay, 1917).

Bhagavad-gītā with the Commentary of Śrī Śaṅkarācārya, trans. by Alladi Mahadeva Sastri (Samanta Books, Madras, 1979).

Bhāmatī of Vācaspati (Nirnayasagar Press, Bombay).

Brahma-siddhi of Maṇḍanamiśra, ed., S. Kuppuswami Sastri (The Madras Government Oriental Manuscripts Series, No. 4, 1937).

Brahma-sūtra of Bādarāyaṇa, with Śaṅkara's Commentary and Sub-commentaries of Gōvindānanda, Vācaspati and Ānandagiri (Nirnayasagar Press, Bombay, 3rd Ed., 1934).

Brahma-sūtra-bhāṣya of Śaṅkara, with text, word-for-word trans. and comments by Swami Vireswarananda (Advaita Ashrama, Calcutta, 1978).

Bṛhadāraṇyaka-upaniṣad-bhāṣya-vārttika of Sureśvara (Ananda Ashrama Sanskrit Series, No. 16).

Iṣṭa-siddhi of Vimuktātman, trans. and notes by P.K. Sundaram (Swadharma Swarajya Sangha, Madras, India 1980).

Kaṭha-upaniṣad-bhāṣya.

Mahābhārata of Kṛṣṇa-dvaipāyana (Veda-vyāsa) (Bangavasi Press, Calcutta, 2nd ed., 1908).

Mahānārāyaṇa Upaniṣad.

Māṇḍūkya Upaniṣad with Gauḍapāda's Kārikā and Śaṅkara's Commentary, text and trans. and annotated by Swami Nikhilananda (Sri Ramakrishna Ashrama, Mysore, 1936).

Mīmāṃsā-sūtra of Jaimini, with Śabara's Commentary (Ananda Ashrama Sanskrit Series, No. 97, in 6 vols., 1933).

Naiṣkarmya-siddhi of Sureśvara (Bombay Sanskrit and Prakrit Series, No. XXXVIII, 1925).

Nṛsiṃhapūrvatāpanīya Upaniṣad.

Pañcadaśī of Vidyāraṇya (Sri Ramakrishna Math, India, 1975).

Pañcapādikā-vivaraṇa of Prakāśātman in Padmapāda's Pañcapādikā (Government Manuscripts Library, Madras, 1958).
Ṛg-veda-saṃhitā with Sāyaṇa's Commentary, ed. by F. Max Müller, 4 vols. (London: Oxford University Press, 1890).
Sambandha-vārttika of Sureśvara, Ed. and trans., T.M.P. Mahadevan (University of Madras, India, 1958).
Saṃkṣepaśārīraka of Sarvajñātman (Madras University Philosophical Series, No. 18, 1985).
Śatadūṣaṇī of Vedānta Deśika, ed. with Tamil translation by Setlur Narasimhachariar (Nigamaparimala Press, 2 vols.).
Siddhāntabindu of Madhusūdana Sarasvatī, Ed., Trayambakam Sastri (Kavi Sanskrit Series, No. 62, 1928).
Śrī-bhāṣya of Rāmānuja (Advaita Ashrama, Calcutta, 1978).
Śrī-śaṅkarāśaṅkara-bhāṣya-vimarṣaḥ of Ramarayakavi (Guntur, 1953).
Śrutaprakāśikā in Rāmānuja's Śrī-bhāṣya with the Commentary Śrutaprakāśikā, ed., T. Srinivasa Sarma (Nirnayasagar Press, Bombay, 1916).
Taittirīya Āraṇyaka with Sāyaṇa's Commentary, 2 parts (Ananda Ashrama Sanskrit Series, Poona, No. 36).
Taittirīya Saṃhitā with Sāyaṇa's Commentary, 3 parts (Ananda Ashrama Sanskrit Series, Poona, No. 37).
Taittirīya-upaniṣad-bhāṣya-vārttika of Sureśvara, Intro. and trans. by R. Balasubramaniam (Madras University Philosophical Series, No. 20, 1984).
Tattvapradīpikā of Citsukha (Nirnayasagar Press, Bombay, 2nd Edn.).
Upaniṣads, The Principal, trans. by S. Radhakrishnan (London: George Allen and Unwin, 1953).
Vedānta-paribhāṣā of Dharmarājādhvarīndra, Trans. by Swami Madhavananda (Advaita Ashrama, Calcutta, 1983).
Vedānta-sāra of Sadānanda Yōgīndra, ed. by Col. G.A. Jacob (Nirnayasagar Press, Bombay, 1925).
Vivaraṇa-prameya-saṅgraha of Bhāratītīrtha Vidyāraṇya, ed. by Ramasastri Tailanga (Vizianagaram Sanskrit Series, No. 7, E.J. Lazarus and Co., Benares, 1893).
Yatīndramatadīpikā of Śrīnivāsadāsa (Sri Ramakrishna Math, India, 1978).

Secondary Sources

Alston, A.J., trans: *Realization of the Absolute*, Shanti Sadan, London, 1971.

Balasubramaniam, R.: *Perspectives of Theism and Absolutism in Indian Philosophy*, Vivekananda College, Madras, 1978.

Jha, G.N.: *Indian Thought*, vol. II, Oriental Book Depot, Poona, 1939.

Mahadevan, T.M.P.: *The Philosophy of Advaita,* Arnold-Heinemann, India, 1976.

Narain, K.: *A Critique of Mādhva Refutation of the Śaṅkara School of Vedānta,* Udayana Publications, Allahabad, 1964.

Radhakrishnan, S.: *Indian Philosophy*, vol. II, Blackie & Son Publishers Pvt. Ltd., India, 1977.

Srinivasachari, P.N.: *The Philosophy of Bhedābheda*, Srinivasa Varadachari and Co., Madras, 1934.

Whitehead, A.N.: *Adventures of Ideas,* University Press, Cambridge, 1933.

INDEX

abheda 16
adhikāri 120
adhyāsa 20, 51-53
advaita: meaning 11-12
akhaṇḍākāra-vṛtti-jñāna 27, 39, 67, 76
Ānandabodha 4
anavasthā 31
anirvacanīya 11, 50, 65, 69, 73
anirvacanīya anupapatti 72-77
antaryāmin 15, 109
anuyogin 88-89
anyonyāśraya 27
apauruṣeya 4, 117
apṛthak-siddhi 13, 19
arcā 15
āśraya anupapatti 27-44
āstika 4
avatāra 15
avidyā and *māyā* 66-67
  key concept 19-23
  nature of 49-50
  role of 19-23
  six aspects 21
  superimposition 67
  two powers 47, 48-49, 51, 80-81
  locus chapter two
    in *jīva* 25, 27-29, 32
    in *Brahman* 25-27, 35-38
    one or many 30
    infinite regress 32
    inexplicability 32-33, 35
    reciprocal dependence 33-34
    defect 34
    no co-existence 36
    types of knowledge 36-38
    not an object of knowledge 39
    removal of knowledge 40
    Brahman not a knower 42
    Brahman self-luminous 42
    Brahman ever-free 42
    Brahman omniscient 42
    in whole or part? 43-44
  obscuration chapter three
    what is it? 45
  nature chapter four
    cognizability 59
    mithya 60-61
    real or not 62-67
  inexplicability chapter five
  not positive chapter six
    root cause 81
    terminable 86
    preception 87-88
    negation 88-90
    inference 92-93
    scripture 94-96
    presumption 96-97
  removability I chapter seven
    has an end 99
    not removable 99
    perception 100-04
    inference 104-05
    verbal testimony 105-12
  removability II chapter eight
    nature of knowledge 116-17

Bādarāyana 1, 7
Bhāskara 3
bheda 103-04
Brahman locus of *avidyā* 35-44
  :five forms 15
  :as content of *avidyā* 49
Brahmānanda 4

causation 81-84
Citśukha 4
cognizability 59-60

dharma-bhūta-jñāna 38
differences: kinds 12
distinctions: between standpoints 9-14
  : between types of metaphysics 14-16
  : between types of scripture 16-18

eka-śāstra 17

ghaṭaka 16

identity statements 106-11
inference 92-94
Īśvara 13, 15, 16, 21, 22, 45, 46, 47, 48, 49, 56,66, 96

Jaimini 1
jāti 101, 104
Jayatīrtha 4
jīva locus of *avidyā* 27-35
  : nature 45
jīvanmukta 23, 48-49
jñāna-kāṇḍa 17-18

karma-kāṇḍa 17-18

Madhva 2
Madhusūdana Sarasvatī 4, 31

Maṇḍana 27, 35
mithyā 11, 83, 114

nāstika 4
nimitta-kāraṇa 13
nirguṇa 15, 25, 43, 83, 105, 109
nirvartaka anupapatti chapter seven
nivṛtti anupapatti chapter eight

para 15
pāramārthika 9, 14, 31, 55, 71
perception 87-91, 100-04
phala-vyāpyatva 76
prakṛti 84, 85, 96, 105, 109
pramāṇa 80
pramāṇa anupapatti chapter six
prasthāna-traya 6
pratiyogin 88-89

Rāmarāyakavi 4

sadasatvilakṣaṇa 11, 70
saguṇa 21
sākṣin 41, 80, 102
samavāya 19
sapta vidhā anupapatti 22, 121
Sarvajñātman 28
Śrī Harṣa 4
Śrī Yāmuna 3
Sudarśana 3, 8, 26, 32
Sureśvara 51
sūtra: definition 1
svarūpa-anupapatti Chapter Four
svarūpa-jñāna 36, 37-38, 55-56, 79, 89, 111

texts: types 16-18
tirodhāna-anupapatti 45-57
tripuṭī 20, 102

upādāna-kāraṇa 13, 84
Upaniṣads 1, 5, 15, 16-17

vārtika definition 7
vāstavī 69
Veda 1, 4-5
vedānta meaning 1, 5
Vedānta Deśika 3, 8, 26, 29-31, 85-86, 91, 117
Veda-vyāsa 5
verbal testimony 105-12
vibhāva 15
Visiṣṭādvaita: 3 realities 12-13
: key concept 13
: definition 13
vivartavāda 20, 22, 84
vṛtti-jñāna 36-37, 55, 79, 111, 116
vṛtti-vyāpyatva 76
Vyāsarāya 4
vyāvahārika 9, 71, 86
vyūha 15